THE SPLENDID BOOK OF THE BICYCLE

THE SPLENDID BOOK OF THE BICYCLE

Daniel Tatarsky

CONTENTS

Title page A 1920 poster of the Michelin Man, who is actually called Bibendum.

Right Wipeout! During a 100 km race at New York in 1923, a nasty pile-up occurs on the first bend.

THE JOY OF CYCLING

There are a number of moments that serve as waypoints in everyone's life. Your first childhood memory, your first day at school, a kiss, a wedding, the birth of a child. But among these memories one remains indelible – the day you first learned to ride a bike.

It is a wonderful moment when balance materialises, fear disappears and you are transported, almost magically, through space and time. It is a moment of growing up – when you put away your childish stabilisers. But it is also the moment when a second childhood begins. Everyone feels younger, happier and freer on a bicycle. Compared to the drudgery of walking, or the complications of a car, bikes offer a form of simple everyday enchantment. Who would think that some metal, some rubber and a chain could offer such a wonderful return on an investment, where pedalling is not a chore but a joy.

And whereas some inventions have fallen by the wayside – the steam train, perhaps soon the internal combustion engine – the bicycle keeps going strong. And stronger. Whereas car and bicycle production were neck and neck until about 1965, with 20 million of each being produced each year, since then bikes have broken from the pack. Since 2003 more than 100 million bikes are produced each year, more than twice the amount of cars. Moreover, bicycles never die. Whereas cars soon become obsolete, and crushed to make way for newer models, bikes are daily being restored by enthusiasts. Their punctures are fixed, their chains lubricated, their handlebars shone: reborn and returned to their former glory, and capable of keeping up with the best of them.

Despite their simplicity, the world of bikes is as wonderful and wide-ranging as life itself. So welcome to *The Splendid Book of the Bicycle*. Here you will learn not only about bikes, but their history, their achievements and what they might one day become. You will explore bicycles in wartime, bicycle aerodynamics, bikes in the movies and the greatest bicycle adventurers of all time. *The Splendid Book of the Bicycle* is a companion to mankind's greatest companion (apart from his dog) – *his bike*.

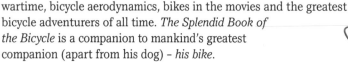

Left An illustration from the Italian Newspaper *La Domenica del Corriere* from 1930: a group of Italian riders from that year's Tour de France.

Below left A classic: the folding BSA paratrooper bike from the Second World War.

PUSHING OFF

HOBBY HORSE TO

When and where the bicycle was first dreamt of is shrouded in the mists of time. The wheel was invented in antiquity, and before that the roller – a smoothed tree trunk – had transported stones to the pyramids and Stonehenge. Carriage and cart technology had improved over the centuries, to the extent that by the mid-1700s passengers enjoyed large, spoked carriage wheels, with steel axle inserts and flat steel tyres. But the drive for improvement that characterised the late eighteenth-century Enlightenment would not stop there. There was an innate faith in the power of reason, and the power of a mechanical world-view. Surely mankind could do better than simply to continue his age-old reliance on the horse?

And it was this belief in the power of human invention that led the German Karl Drais to invent, in 1817, the *Laufmaschine* (running machine). Drais was a German aristocrat with radical sympathies, who was to go on to support the Revolution of 1848. He was also a prolific inventor, inventing a typewriter, a music recording machine and a meat grinder. But it is his pioneering Hobby Horse that has become his most lasting legacy.

Drais's innovation was to relinquish the obsession with two- or three-wheeled machines that were driven by hand-cranks, all of which were underpowered and difficult to steer. Drais realised that a two-wheeled machine could be balanced by small modifications in steering, and steered using greater deviations. In effect Drais provided a form of heightened walking, or running, with the strong muscles of the legs providing power, but the wheels providing a boost to forward motion. As with all great inventions it was simple, but powerful - as can be seen in the way the design lives on in modern balance bikes designed for toddlers.

And as with all great inventions it was soon imitated. The following year Denis Johnson of London had copied but improved on Drais's original, adding footrests and smoother lines. And soon in both France and England, Drais's invention had become all the rage among young fashionable aristocrats, becoming known as the *Draisienne* or *velocipede* (fast feet) in France, and the Hobby Horse or Dandy Horse (because unlike a real horse it did not require constant maintenance) in England. Cartoons soon ridiculed this new aristocratic fad. One cartoon entitled 'Anti Dandy Infantry triumphant - or the Velocipede Cavalry Unhobbey'd', showed a blacksmith, fearful for his job, smashing up one of the offending vehicles, and a vet, fearful for his employment too, administering a large lethal syringe to the crashed rider. In the background a dog chases another hobby-

BONESHAKER

A gentlemanly cadence: Johnson's Pedestrian Hobby Horse of 1819, with a speeding rider in the background.

horser into the distance. Despite its unpopularity among members of the non-riding public, the bicycle (of sorts) had arrived.

The Boneshaker, the next stage in the bicycle's evolution, was a natural progression from the Hobby Horse. In fact, the story goes that in 1861 the Parisian blacksmith Pierre Micheaux was repairing a Hobby Horse in his workshop when he decided to fit pedals and cranks to the front wheel. (Other accounts stress the role of Pierre Lallement, a baby carriage manufacturer from Nancy, who filed a patent for a similar design in 1866.)

Micheaux's design came to be called a 'boneshaker' because unlike the Hobby Horse, all the rider's weight was placed on the saddle, rather than also being conveyed to the ground via the legs. It was in some ways unstable as the power applied to the pedal had a tendency to twist the front wheel to one side. The ride

Above An elegant Boneshaker. See the concessions to comfort with the sprung saddle compensating for the solid wheels, and the safety measures of a light and back brake. **Right** How do you drive this thing? An early Boneshaker novice summons up courage.

was a rough one, with wooden wheels and iron tyres rattling along the cobbled streets of nineteenth-century France. But there were some concessions to comfort – via a sprung seat, lubricated brass bearings – and safety, in the form of a rudimentary brake: a wooden pad pressed against the rear wheel. A print from 1869 shows a Boneshaker outpacing a horse, with the caption: 'We can beat the swiftest steed, With our new velocipede'.

Micheaux's Bicycle Company was formed in 1868, producing bicycles at the rate of five a day, and the design soon caught on. Other manufacturers carried out their own innovations. The Scotsman Thomas McCall powered the rear wheels by a system of cranks linked to the pedals, trying to obviate the need for the Boneshaker rider to sit almost astride the front wheel. Other manufacturers introduced metal rather than wooden spokes, and shod their bikes with solid rubber wheels. By 1869, Boneshakers were being produced in their thousands. The bicycle proper had been born, converting the up-and-down motion of walking into the cyclical motion of the wheel.

PENNY FARTHING OR ORDINARY BICYCLE

Micheaux's Boneshaker was a revolution in human transport. But it still faced problems. One was simply the ride – on a smooth road it was tolerable, but on a cobbled street it was torture. The other was its speed. As the cranks were directly connected to the front wheel, speed was limited by the cadence (number of revolutions) that human legs were capable of (think of how furiously a child has to pedal a tricycle in order to move with any sort of speed). A normal cycling cadence is around 60 revolutions per minute. With the cranks directly connected to the wheel on, say, a wheel the size of a modern mountain bike (26 inches in diameter) you could reach only five miles an hour – little more than walking speed. So the problem was that the Boneshaker was an improvement over walking, especially down hills, but not by much.

Hence the arrival of the Ordinary Bicycle, High-Wheeler or Penny Farthing. At first it looks anything but ordinary, like the perfect symbol of Victorian eccentricity: austere men with beards and splendid moustaches perched atop absurdly precarious follies of bicycles. It may have allowed them to peer over the tops of hedgerows but it was absolutely lethal in a crash - what came to be called a 'header'. Absurd as they may have seemed, the design of the Ordinary served an important function: it increased the speed of bicycling, to the extent that in 1876 Frank Dodds cycled for an hour around the Cambridge University athletics track, clocking up an average speed of 15.8 miles an hour. This record was broken by Frederick Osmond in 1891, who cycled 23 miles in an hour. With the Penny Farthing, the bicycle became less of an aristocratic fad, and more a means of transport: of covering distances efficiently and reliably in good time.

Right Reflections on bicycle history. The motorcycle racer George Greenwood rides a Penny Farthing around Wembley Stadium in 1935. **Left** A sporting 'wheelman' and high wheeler in 1875. Note the aerodynamic moustache.

As with many moments in bicycle design, the French played a key role. In 1868, Eugène Meyer received a patent for a wire-spoked bicycle and in the following year assembled a wire-spoked High-Wheeler. The tensioned spokes meant that a wheel could be built lightly, but strongly, its size only limited by the inside leg of the rider. Now wheel sizes could increase without becoming unwieldy, growing to 48 inches through to 60 inches for the tallest riders.

As before, this cycling innovation was quickly imitated. French High-Wheelers brought to England were soon copied by English manufacturers. In 1870, James Starley patented the 'Ariel' – named after the airy-light spirit of Shakespeare's *The Tempest* – the first mass-produced all-metal bicycle, which earned Starley a

SOME PENNY FARTHING RECORDS

1885

Will Robertson rode a 'Star' bicycle – a model with the smaller wheel in front – down the steps of the U.S. Senate building in Washington.

1886

George P. Mills cycled from Lands End to John O'Groats in 5 days, 1 hour and 45 minutes. He slept for only six hours during the trip.

1886

W. J. Morgan of Minneapolis cycled for 234 miles without getting off his bicycle.

reputation as the father of the bicycle industry. The Ariel was advertised as 'the lightest, strongest, and most elegant of modern bicycles'. What was key was the tensioned spokes of the front wheel, over which much of the rider's weight was carried. Tensioned spokes allowed the wheel to be even lighter than the first high-wheeler, but unlike solid spokes – as on a cartwheel – they also allowed for a degree of shock absorption. This was improved further by Starley's invention, in 1874, of tangential spokes – spokes set at an angle to the radius of the wheel, crossing each other before they reached the hub. By this system of bracing, the wheel was able to resist not only the vertical weight of the rider and machine, but the twisting force that transmitted power from the cranks, via the spokes to the rims. As a final luxury, Starley added solid rubber tyres. Wheels could therefore be lightweight, strong and shock-absorbing, but also tuned by tightening the spokes to keep them true, a design innovation that continues in nearly all modern bicycles.

Starley and Meyer's design soon caught on. By 1875 High-Wheelers or, as they came to be known, Penny Farthings (after the large and small coins they resembled), were being manufactured in the tens of thousands by 30 manufacturers in the U.K, increasing to 400,000 bicycles and 22 manufacturers in 1885. Many of them emerged from the sewing machine industry in Coventry, with names like Singer, Swift and Phoenix. Bikes were shaking off their bone-shaking reputation and beginning to be associated with lightness, comfort and speed.

Left Those were the days. A biscuit-fuelled excursion in the 1870s, with a lady aboard a tricycle bringing up the rear.

Below An early boy band called 'The Penny Farthings' pose while on tour in the 1890s.

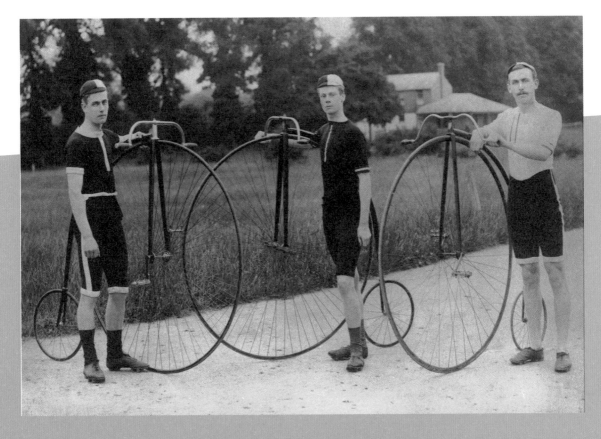

THE BIRTH OF THE SAFETY BICYCLE

The Safety Bicycle was developed as an antidote to the lack of safety of the Ordinary Bicycle or Penny Farthing. We've already seen how its high centre of gravity above the huge front wheel made the Ordinary liable to create a journey fraught with danger. To make cycling safer it was necessary to go back to the drawing board and, while keeping all the basic components of wheels, pedals, seat and handle bars, creating something game-changingly different.

Let's take each of those elements and examine how the Safety Bicycle adapted them to make life in the saddle more fun and less hazardous.

THE PEDALS The advance here is not actually in the pedals themselves but in how they are used to drive the bicycle. Rather than simply turning the enormous front wheel, the pedals were moved to the centre of the cycle and drove the rear wheel by a chain. By having a chainring with a larger diameter than that of the sprocket on the rear wheel, a positive gear ratio is created, meaning that a single rotation of the pedals would result in a greater number of rotations of the wheel.

THE WHEELS The Safety had two wheels of the same size and this resulted in a fundamental reduction in the likelihood of injury. Firstly, it meant that the cyclist could put their feet on the ground when the bike was stationary. Immediately this made starting and stopping much easier. You could start with a foot down, creating three points of contact with the ground and a much more stable situation. The same was true of stopping. Secondly, on stopping, there was much less likelihood of the rider's momentum taking them over the front wheel. This was also linked to the change in the saddle's position.

Right John Kemp Starley riding his Rover Safety Bicycle.

THE FRAME The Penny Farthing didn't have a frame as such. It was more a structure that held the two wheels in place. The diamond frame was the core of the safety bike and gave it one of its other names (the Diamond). It is, in effect, two triangles either side of the seat post. Both triangles have as one side the line from the saddle to the chainring. One then extends from those two points to the axis of the front wheel and the other to the axis of the rear wheel. These two triangles form a diamond shape.

THE HANDLEBARS By placing these level with the saddle and above the axis of the front wheel, the cyclist is forced into a position that is more stable for controlling the bike and is more able to deliver force efficiently to the pedals.

THE CHAIN Without the chain the safety bicycle would not have happened. It is the chain which allowed the pedals to be moved off the front wheel and was in effect the catalyst for the whole development. We should therefore give thanks to Hans Renold, the inventor of the driving or roller chain.

THE SADDLE By bringing the centre of gravity lower and further back on the machine, between the two wheels, everything became more stable. Going over the handlebars (taking a 'header') was a major problem on the Penny Farthing, but on the Safety this became much less likely.

These developments and innovations created a bicycle that has remained practically unchanged for over 125 years. The first Safety Bicycle was manufactured in the 1870s, give or take a decade (we'll come to that in a moment), but it would not look out of place on your high street today.

There are two people who are, above all others, held to be the 'fathers' of the Safety Bicycle. First up is Henry John Lawson, known as Harry, born in London in 1852, the son of a brass turner. In the early 1870s he was working in Brighton with James Likeman on lever-driven cycles, but later that decade the two of them jointly applied for patents for what would become the Safety. This bike has been recognised as the first to actually be made using a rear wheel that was chain driven, although the front wheel was still about twice the diameter of the rear.

While Lawson manufactured the first recognisable Safety Bicycle, it was John Kemp Starley who designed and manufactured the first bike that reached a mass market and made cycling the most common and affordable form of transport available. His father James had set the path for the family business with his Ariel, which was of a Penny Farthing design, and kicked off cycle manufacturing in this country. When John Kemp Starley produced the Rover Safety Bicycle in 1885, his place in history was set. It is this bike that made the mould and was a massive success all over the world.

The Rover was the first mass-produced, commercially successful Safety Bicycle, and it quickly became an important means of transport.

GEAR RATIOS EXPLAINED

Gear ratios are calculated by comparing the number of the teeth on the chainring (input) and the sprocket (output). If the chainring has 40 teeth and the sprocket has 10 teeth the ratio is 4 to 1. One full turn of the pedals will result in four turns of the wheel. You can go the other way so 40 teeth on the chainring with 50 on the sprockets gives a ratio of 4 to 5, this would require the pedals to go round more than once to get a full rotation of the wheel. This is what you want when setting off, or going uphill.

THE ROVER SAFETY BICYCLE (PATENTED).

BRADLEY BIRMᴺ

Safer than any Tricycle, faster and easier than any Bicycle ever made. Fitted with handles to turn for convenience in storing or shipping. Far and away the best hill-climber in the market.

MANUFACTURED BY

STARLEY & SUTTON,

METEOR WORKS, WEST ORCHARD, COVENTRY, ENGLAND.

Price Lists of "Meteor, "Rover," "Despatch," and "Sociable" Bicycles and Tricycles, and the "Coventry Chair," Illustrated, free on application.

CARS AND BIKES

H.J. Lawson founded the Daimler Motor Company. In 1904, three years after his death, J.K. Starley's Rover Cycle Company moved into cars.

WHAT MAKES A BIKE
THE NAMING OF PARTS

If you took your bike apart, every little bit, and laid all the pieces end to end, it would cover a distance of almost 50 metres! Here's a handy guide.

❶ **SADDLE** The main difference in saddle design comes between racing and non-racing bikes. For the former, where the rider is generally leaning further forward and thus spreading their weight more evenly between the saddle and the handlebars, cushioning is less. Generally the saddle should be adjusted to be parallel to the ground. The saddle is held to the seatpost by the seat rail and seat clamp.

❷ **SEATPOST** This holds the saddle in place and fits into the seat tube. It's adjustable for height. The ideal height is where, with your legs hanging relaxed and straight, your heel just touches the pedal at its lowest position.

❸ **SEATPOST CLAMP** This holds the seatpost in place once you have adjusted the height.

The seatpost fits into the seat tube, which is part of the **frame**. While it is one piece, the frame has several elements.

Frame

❹ **TOP TUBE** goes from the seat tube to the handlebars.

❺ **SEAT TUBE** runs from the seat down to the crank set. It splits the diamond in two, making two triangles.

❻ **SEAT STAYS** run from the top of the seat tube to the axis of the rear wheel.

❼ **CHAIN STAYS** run from the axis of the rear wheel to the pedals.

❽ **DOWN TUBE** runs up from the pedals towards the handlebars.

❾ **HEAD TUBE** joins the top and down tubes just below the handlebars.

❿ **FORKS** run down from the head tube to the axis of the front wheel.

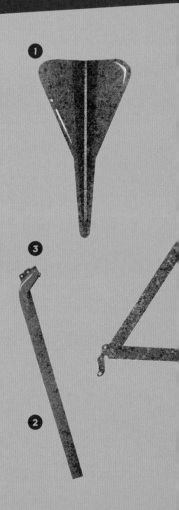

It all gets a little bit *Dem Bones* now with bits connected to bits, but stick with it.

⑪ HEAD SET A short attachment to the head tube which holds the...

⑫ STEM Another small tube which holds the...

⑬ HANDLEBARS After all those tubes and stays, finally something that seems familiar. There are basically two types of handlebar and all the others are variants of this. There's the drop handlebar, which loops forward and down. This is the sort you'd see on a racing bike. You can either lean all the way forward and hold the far edge of the loop or you can sit up and hold the top of the loop. The other main type is the standard that is on most road bikes. They just come straight out from the stem and may curl backwards. These will have the rider sitting in a more upright position. Attached to the handlebars are two things vital to the bike.

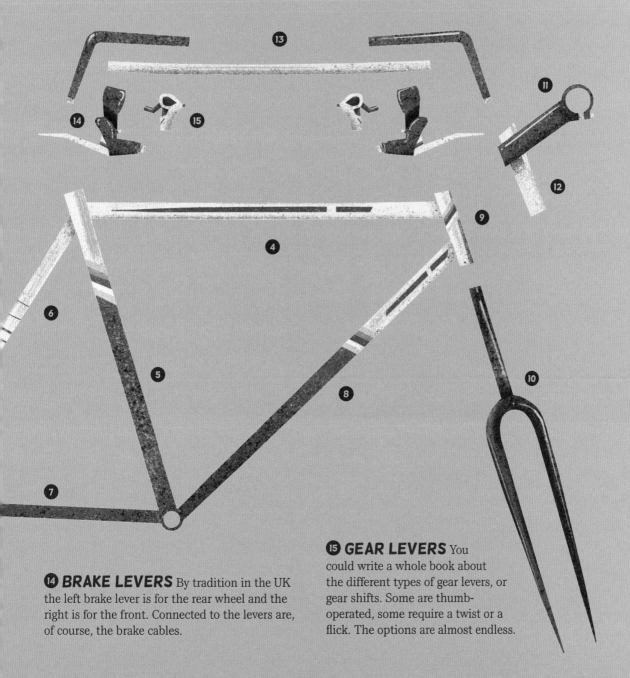

⑭ BRAKE LEVERS By tradition in the UK the left brake lever is for the rear wheel and the right is for the front. Connected to the levers are, of course, the brake cables.

⑮ GEAR LEVERS You could write a whole book about the different types of gear levers, or gear shifts. Some are thumb-operated, some require a twist or a flick. The options are almost endless.

16 BRAKES Operated by the brake levers via the brake cable, there are three main types of brake. With **rim** brakes, pads are pressed against the wheel rim; with **disc** brakes, pads are pressed against a metal disc around the wheel hub; and with **drum** brakes, pads are pressed outwards against the hub shell.

17 FRONT WHEEL Starting from the middle we have the **hub**: this sits in the **dropout** at the end of the fork. Emanating from the hub are the **spokes** that are attached to the **rim** by **nipples**. These nipples can be adjusted to change the tension in the spokes. Inside the rim of the wheel there is a tough nylon or rubber strip which protects the **inner tube** from the nipples. Coming through a hole in the rim from the inner tube is the **valve**. This is the conduit, if you like, for putting air into the inner tube.

Most road bikes will have **mudguards** around the front and rear wheels. These prevent water and dirt picked up by the tyre from the road being thrown upwards and onto the rider's back.

18 REAR WHEEL This is, in the main, the same as the front but has a lot more furniture around, namely the **gears**.

Gears

There are two main types of gear mechanism, external and internal. The difference is that with the former all the mechanics can be seen, while the latter holds everything within a drum.

⑲ EXTERNAL GEARS This mechanism consists of two main parts. The **cassette** is a single unit made up of a number of **sprocketed cogs** of varying size; the **derailleur** is connected beneath the cassette. Its job is to shift the chain between the cogs, thus changing the gear ratio.

⑳ INTERNAL GEARS Contained within a hub is a **planetary gear** which, in its simplest form, consists of three elements: **the sun gear**, the **planetary gear** and the **internal gear**.

Last but not least is the engine. The bit that actually makes it all go and is the way that the rider's energy is transmitted to the bike.

㉑ PEDALS This is where you place your feet and propel the bike. The pedals are attached to...

㉒ CRANKS and the **CRANKSET** The cranks make the crankset rotate when the rider applies pressure to the pedals. Within the crankset is the **chainring** which, with sprockets, holds the **chain** and transfers the rider's energy to the back wheel.

And now that you've taken your bike apart and named all the pieces lying at your feet, all you have to do is put it back together and pedal off into the setting sun.

PNEUMATIC EXPERIMENTS
DUNLOP AND THE CUSHIONED RIDE

The Safety Bicycle made cycling less dangerous – but it was still rather uncomfortable. The ride was not as bad as it had been on the very first bikes, which had a ribbon of iron encasing a wooden wheel. Every lump and bump was communicated straight up to the rider's posterior and from there through their whole body. 'Boneshaker' was a very apt name. It is thanks to two pioneers from the first half of the nineteenth century and one from the second half that we can now ride on almost any terrain without having our skeleton shaken up.

The Glaswegian Charles Macintosh is credited with developing the waterproof raincoat in the early 1820s. He gave it his name and it is now commonly known as the Mackintosh, or Mac. The vital ingredient in his invention was India rubber. The substance had been used in India for waterproofing but it was Macintosh who saw its value to people living in rainy Scotland and beyond. His breakthrough was in making the rubber more pliable, but even in this form, in extreme temperatures it tended to suffer, becoming sticky in the heat and brittle in the cold.

The next step, or turn of the wheel, came courtesy of Charles Goodyear. He was awarded the U.S. patent for his vulcanised rubber in 1844. The process involved changing the properties of natural rubber by adding sulphur. This overcame the stickiness and brittleness problems encountered with rubber in its natural state. A nod of the bicycle helmet should also, at this point, go to Thomas Hancock of Wiltshire in the U.K. Goodyear was more interested in developing different uses for his vulcanised rubber, but it was Hancock who invented the machinery for actually processing it.

It was vulcanised rubber that was used as the first improvement on the metal tyres on wooden wheels. In the first instance these tyres were solid rubber. It was

Left John Boyd Dunlop lived to the ripe old age of 81 and his pneumatic tyres kept him comfortable to the end.

Below Dunlop's son was the inspiration for and one of the first beneficiaries of air-filled tyres.

flexible and strong and was certainly an improvement on the Boneshakers - but it was not the end of the story.

Our third and final pioneer is the Scotsman John Boyd Dunlop. While Macintosh and Goodyear were both chemists and could therefore have been expected to do the work they did, Dunlop's contribution came from left-field as he was a veterinary surgeon. This profession took him to Belfast and it was here in the late 1880s that he invented the first pneumatic tyre. They say that necessity is the mother of invention, and this is a classic case in point. His son Johnnie complained to him about the lack of comfort when cycling his tricycle on the cobbled and rough streets of Belfast. Around the same time, as part of his veterinary work, he had been working on an air-cushioned collar for horses pulling heavy cargo on the city's streets.

Dunlop made the tube by gluing together two strips of rubber. He covered this with linen and stuck it to a wooden disc. And thus was the first pneumatic tyre

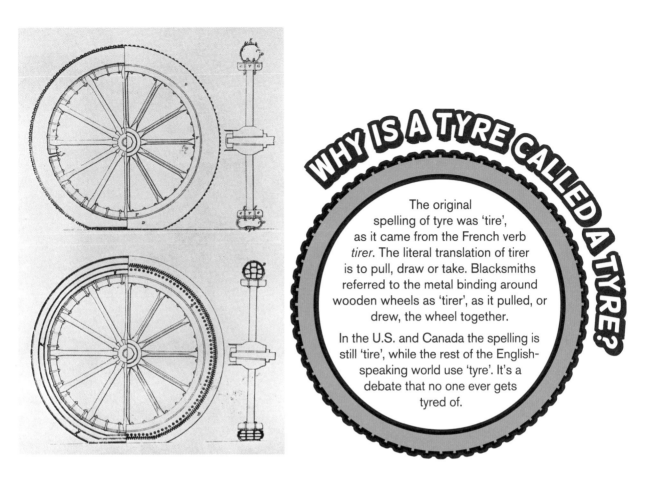

The original spelling of tyre was 'tire', as it came from the French verb *tirer*. The literal translation of tirer is to pull, draw or take. Blacksmiths referred to the metal binding around wooden wheels as 'tirer', as it pulled, or drew, the wheel together.

In the U.S. and Canada the spelling is still 'tire', while the rest of the English-speaking world use 'tyre'. It's a debate that no one ever gets tyred of.

invented. This all happened at the end of 1887 and by December 1888 Dunlop had patented his invention – and revolutionised cycling.

There's a much used expression regarding reinventing the wheel, often used to knock new ideas that do the same thing as something already in use. For John Boyd Dunlop, he really did reinvent the wheel, or the tyre at least, because it turned out he'd been beaten to the pneumatic tyre invention by a fellow Scot, Robert William Thomson. Thomson was granted a patent for his 'improvement in carriage-wheels' in 1847, and his application makes it quite clear that his is a pneumatic tyre: 'a hollow belt composed of some air and water tight material, such as sulphurised caoutchouc [...] and inflating it with air'. It may have been because this patent was granted in the U.S., or simply because forty years later no-one had taken it up and done anything with it, but Dunlop was granted his patent for pretty much the same thing. His name is written in history even though Dunlop's patent was made invalid when the duplication was brought to the patent office's attention.

These days there is a divide between the type of tyre used by the everyday rider and those professionals who make their living from cycling. For those who cycle to work, or just for fun, the standard type of tyre is a clincher. This is a tyre that is held on to the rim of the wheel by beading. Inside this tyre, and protected by it, is a separate inner tube. The pro uses a tubular tyre. This is where the tyre and the inner tube are joined together and attached to the wheel, and held in place, by glue. This type of tyre is much harder and slower to repair but due to its reduced weight it is preferred for racing.

Above Drawings from Robert William Thomson's patent application in 1845.

Left An advertising poster for Dunlop tyres; the first manufactured pneumatic tyre that revolutionised cycling.

VICTORIAN TRICK

The music hall and the circus were at the heart of Victorian popular culture. Sketches and songs reflected the realities of working-class existence – lodgers, bailiffs and overdue rent. Clowns served as a distraction from the mechanical repetition of life on the factory floor. But it was not long before bicycles began to feature as one of the most popular speciality acts on the Victorian stage – a more benign mixing of man and machine to star alongside the traditional mix of animals, dancers and strongmen.

CYCLISTS

Acts included such stunts as a boy doing a wheelie with another smaller boy on his shoulders, and a man balancing his bike on two candles. The American stuntman Robert Vandervoort – 'Il Diavolo' – was the first to complete a loop-the-loop on a bike on Coney Island in 1902. On a specially adapted bike, with no pedals or brakes, Vandervoort descended a wooden ramp, before cycling upside down through the 40-foot hoop. The *Clinton Morning Age* reported in April 1902:

> *With no other aid than the velocity accumulated by a rush down a steep incline the man rode up the concave surface until he hung head downward and continued on down out of the loop to dismount, cool and collected, 100 feet away.*

Vandervoort toured the world with his act and performed a command performance before King Edward VII in London in May 1903.

Other less daring acts combined music and cycling, and these included The Cycling Elliots and the Musical Savonas with their bicycles and saxophones. Sometimes acts combined athleticism with the eroticism of the circus. Around the turn of the century Kaufmann's Cycling Beauties wowed audiences not only with their synchronised pedalling but also their skin-tight cycling outfits, looking like embroidered velodrome riders before their time with floral bonnets instead of helmets.

Trick cycling was not limited to the professionals. In 1901 Isobel Marks published *Fancy Cycling: Trick Cycling for Amateurs*. Here the unflappable Miss Marks gave sober instruction on how to liven up any Edwardian garden party once the cucumber sandwiches had run out. Her aim was to: 'give an account of the many graceful, daring, and altogether fascinating feats which may be accomplished by any rider possessed of an ordinary amount of nerve'. And nerve was something that the war-bound Edwardians possessed in abundance.

Tricks included such classics as the 'Butterfly Dance' – flapping a single sheet while riding no-handed, 'Riding on one wheel' – the wheelie as it is now known, and 'Riding backwards sitting on the handlebars' – the key here was folding one's arms to create a sense of the necessary insouciance. But perhaps

Above Sheer skills: a Victorian ladies trick cycling display team.

Left Keith's Bicycle Track. Cyclists performing on a bicycle track on stage at Keith's Union Square Theater, New York, *c.*1901.

UPON AN ORDINARY ROAD BICYCLE, DASHING DOWN A GIANT STAIRWAY FROM THE MADISON SQUARE GARDEN ROOF TO THE GROUND BELOW, A SHEER DESCENT OF OVER ONE HUNDRED FEET

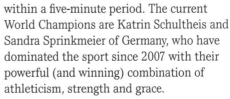
the most artlessly entertaining trick was the 'Hoop skipping'. Here the rider rode no-handed holding a large wooden hoop, which she then passed under the front wheel. Miss Marks continued: 'This effected, a nimble turn of the hoop slants the hoop towards the back wheel, beneath which it slips. It is then raised above the head to recommence the series of operations.'

Key to all of these tricks was keeping a straight face. No matter how daunting, death-defying or daft the trick was, it was imperative than one maintained a certain decorum. Men wore tweeds and hombergs rather than helmets and lycra. Women wore voluminous skirts and corsets. And if one's decorum accidently slipped, Isobel told you how it could be restored. There are sections on 'Removing one's Jacket', and 'Picking up a Handkerchief' - the favourite stunt of many an Edwardian gallant, but this time given a certain spin.

Perhaps predictably, trick cycling never caught on among the English upper classes. But in Germany, the story was different. There the sport of 'Artistic Cycling' became well established and still lives on today. Here cyclists, singly or in pairs, sometimes two to a bike, carry out gymnastic and acrobatic moves to music in an arena 10 metres square. Typically they carry out 30 different moves within a five-minute period. The current World Champions are Katrin Schultheis and Sandra Sprinkmeier of Germany, who have dominated the sport since 2007 with their powerful (and winning) combination of athleticism, strength and grace.

And of course trick cycling as an entertainment, rather than a sport, lives on. Perhaps the most irrepressibly talented trick cyclist in history has to be the fantastically skilled Japanese–American Lilly Yokoi - known as 'The Ballerina on the Golden Bicycle' - who thrilled audiences through the sixties and seventies. Film clips from the time record her wonderful act. She vaults around her gold-plated bike as she careers in a circle, wearing sheer tights and a golden leotard. She plucks off the handlebars and cycles one-footed. She stops the bike then wheelies backwards in a circle. And as a finale - with drum roll and crashing cymbals - turns dozens of pirouettes on the back wheel, before dismounting with an elegant bow.

Lilly embodies all of the glitz and glamour of the sixties but also the wonder of the essence of the bicycle: the joy of human and machine in perfect harmony, together greater than the sum of their parts.

ICONIC BIKES

The Moulton

Can you reinvent the wheel? Probably not. Can you reinvent the bicycle? Maybe. That was certainly the challenge Dr Alex Moulton set himself in 1962, taking on decades of established bicycle design.

Moulton came from an industrial background, his family owned a rubber company, and he studied engineering at Cambridge University. After the family business was bought out he established a new company, Moulton Developments Ltd, in the late fifties. Its first job was the development of the 'Hydrolastic' rubber suspension for the Mini, the iconic car of the sixties designed by Moulton's friend, Sir Alec Issigonis. The revolutionary new suspension did much to inspire Moulton in his creation of an equally revolutionary new bicycle design.

As a reaction to the increased oil prices caused by the Suez Crisis in the late fifties, people turned again to the virtues of cycling, after a long period of decline. However, Moulton recognised that people were put off bicycles by the difficulty of getting on one, the high centre of gravity and harsh ride. In addition, the large wheels made bicycles difficult to store, particularly in the high-rise apartment blocks that were mushrooming up across Britain. He set out to design a comfortable, small-wheeled version that would have mass appeal.

Small wheels, however, tended to have a higher rolling resistance, and offered less shock absorption. Fatter tyres increased comfort, but slowed the bike down. Moulton thus designed small, high pressure 16-inch wheels and tyres, and overcame the problem of a harsh ride through front and rear suspension. It was all mounted on an F-frame design where the handlebar and seat stem emerged from one single spar. At the rear of the frame an integrated rear rack carried luggage.

The revolutionary design of the M1 F-Frame Moulton was launched at the Earls Court Motor Show in 1962 and was an immediate hit. This new, colourful, unisex design of the Moulton captured the youthful irreverence of the swinging sixties, and to this day retains a cult following.

The Dawes Galaxy

What is the greatest bicycle of all time? The original Safety Bicycle, which survives in the DNA of most modern bikes? The Raleigh Roadster, imitated millions of times worldwide? In terms of its achievement in traversing the globe, it may be that redoubtable workhorse of a touring bike, the Dawes Galaxy.

Introduced in 1971, the Dawes Galaxy is more of a constellation of bikes than a single machine, featuring such variants as the Galaxy Plus, Super Galaxy, Ultra Galaxy and the Galaxy tandem Twin. But at the heart of the bikes are the same principles: a long wheelbase, strengthened frame, quality components and a readiness to face roads in any part of the world and at any time of the year.

The Dawes Company of Birmingham - the home of English cycling - began in 1906 when Charles Dawes and Ernie Humphries started making motorbikes. Twenty years later, Dawes set up on his own as a bicycle manufacturer, passing the business onto his son, Wilfred, in 1930. The company soon gained a reputation for making quality cycles and offering unparalleled customer service.

At the 1951 Festival of Britain, Dawes unveiled the 'Courier': a lightweight bike ideal for cycle touring. The 'Windrush' followed, a more highly specified touring model. These were forebears of the world-conquering Galaxy, introduced in 1971. Whereas previously tourers were often expensive custom-made machines, the Galaxy offered an affordable, off-the-shelf solution. Its beating heart was the Reynolds 531 tubing used for the hand-built frame. This manganese-molybdenum, medium-carbon steel gave the frame strength but also flexibility, which combined with the long wheelbase, and relaxed geometry, easily absorbed the shocks of foreign roads.

Since then, Galaxys have been around the world many times and are still in production. A reminder of the virtues of the original were seen in Clare Balding's 2010 television series *Britain by Bike*, where she followed the path of the journalist and bicycling guide author, Harold Briercliffe, pedalling her way round Britain on Briercliffe's own Dawes touring bike.

BOLDLY GOING

AROUND THE WORLD ON A BICYCLE
THE EXTRAORDINARY THOMAS STEVENS

Thomas Stevens was the first man to circumnavigate the globe on a bicycle – not on a relatively modern Safety Bicycle, but on a Penny Farthing.

Stevens was born in Berkhamsted in 1854, but emigrated to America in 1871. There he found work in a railroad mill, and also became a familiar face at San Francisco cycling clubs. He acquired a 50-inch wheel Columbia 'Standard' Penny Farthing, and on 22 April 1884 decided to cycle around the world. He travelled light: some spare socks and a shirt, a raincoat that served as a tent, a bedroll and a .38 Smith & Wesson. A contemporary described him as 'A man of medium height, wearing an oversized blue flannel shirt over blue overalls, which were tucked into a pair of leggings at the knee.' His complexion was as tanned as a nut, and it goes without saying that a handlebar moustache 'protruded from his face'.

Stevens followed the established California Trail that had carried generations of migrants and fortune seekers across the great plains to the Golden State over the course of the nineteenth century. The going was tough, and Stevens was forced to walk a third of the way. But he also took time to record the plight of the native American population that was rapidly dwindling:

Thomas Stevens

KELLY .87

The heroic Thomas
Stevens setting off
with army helmet,
supplies and a
moustache.

I pass a small camp of Digger Indians, to whom my bicycle
is as much a mystery as was the first locomotive; yet they
scarcely turn their uncovered heads to look; and my cheery
greeting of "How," scarce elicits a grunt and a stare in
reply. Long years of chronic hunger and wretchedness
have well-nigh eradicated what little energy these Diggers
ever possessed. The discovery of gold among their native
mountains has been their bane . . .

Stevens journeyed on, coyotes sneaking around him, as he followed the path of the Truckee River, and pressed onwards into the desert. 3,700 miles later, after wagon trails, railways, towpaths and roads, he arrived in Boston, his journey thus far having taken 103 days.

Stevens spent the winter in Boston, before boarding *The City of Chicago* bound for Liverpool, sharing the ship with a company of actors who were returning from a tour. A few weeks later, he departed from Liverpool with members of the Anfield Cycling Club providing a guard of honour.

Stevens rode 'joyously southward along smooth, macadamized highways', passing through the picturesque towns and villages of Cheshire, Staffordshire and into the home counties, sporting a white American army helmet as headgear. England, he concluded, 'is the natural paradise of 'cyclers'. As he approached Watford he was met by the Captain of the North London Tricycle Club.

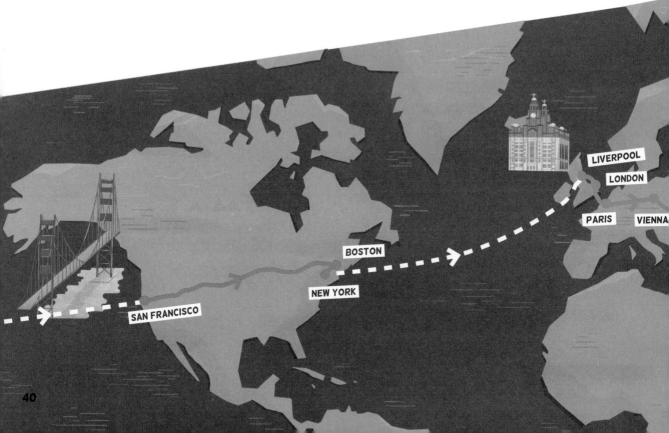

In London he met Major Thomas Knox Holmes, the 'King of British Cycling', who had recently cycled 114 miles in ten hours at the age of 78. He trundled on to Brighton, visiting the Aquarium before setting off for the port of Newhaven. As he set sail for Dieppe, he looked back fondly on his English journey: 'Among other agreeable things to be ever remembered...is the fact that it is the first three hundred miles of road I ever remember riding over without scoring a header'.

After a quibble over paying duty on his bike at Dieppe, Stevens now pressed on through France, 'down the beautiful Arques Valley' in Normandy, 'over roads that are simply perfect for wheeling'. He passed through Rouen, Fontenay and Strasbourg, and from there into Germany - Tubingen, Altheim and Vienna. Then Hungary, Serbia, Bulgaria, Turkey before crossing into what was for many Europeans the uncharted lands of Asia. He spent the winter as a guest of the Shah of Iran, where Stevens gave him a demonstration of his bike's abilities, cycling at speed around the Palace gardens.

After getting expelled from Afghanistan on suspicion of being a Russian spy, Stevens set off again. As he peered over the boat rail, he reflected on how the presence of his bike rendered himself, rather than the country he was visiting, exotic - the observer becoming the observed:

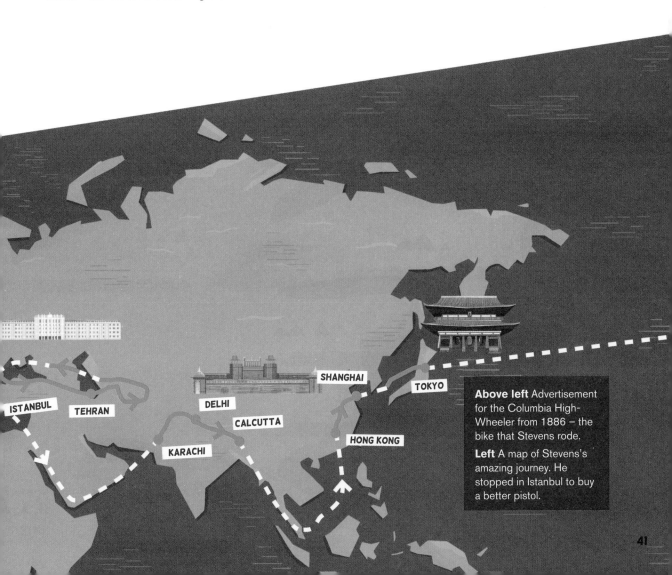

ISTANBUL
TEHRAN
DELHI
CALCUTTA
KARACHI
SHANGHAI
TOKYO
HONG KONG

Above left Advertisement for the Columbia High-Wheeler from 1886 – the bike that Stevens rode.

Left A map of Stevens's amazing journey. He stopped in Istanbul to buy a better pistol.

These people are evidently fascinated by the strange and mysterious manner of my coming among them; who am I, what am I, and wherefore my marvellous manner of travelling, are questions that appeal strongly to their Asiatic imagination, and they are intensely loath to see me disappear again without having seen more of me and my wonderful iron horse, and learned more about it.

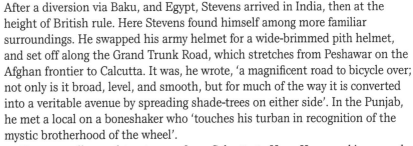

Below A moment of respite: Thomas Stevens stops for a tea party in Japan.

Below right Stevens is surrounded by a mob in China, angry at China's war with France, but also thinking that Stevens was a sorcerer who had caused their crops to fail.

After a diversion via Baku, and Egypt, Stevens arrived in India, then at the height of British rule. Here Stevens found himself among more familiar surroundings. He swapped his army helmet for a wide-brimmed pith helmet, and set off along the Grand Trunk Road, which stretches from Peshawar on the Afghan frontier to Calcutta. It was, he wrote, 'a magnificent road to bicycle over; not only is it broad, level, and smooth, but for much of the way it is converted into a veritable avenue by spreading shade-trees on either side'. In the Punjab, he met a local on a boneshaker who 'touches his turban in recognition of the mystic brotherhood of the wheel'.

He eventually caught a steamer from Calcutta to Hong Kong, and journeyed with some difficulty through Southern China. He was jostled by an angry crowd – his 'coat-tail is jerked, the bicycle stopped, my helmet knocked off'. He frequently got lost. And he became embroiled in a riot, losing a few spokes, before being saved by the local magistrate. By comparison Japan was an island of calm. There the American Consul entertained him before he set off on the final leg of his journey, and despite a collision with a bobtailed cat, he arrived at Yokohama on 17 December 1886, and boarded a steamship to San Francisco and home.

Stevens' journey remains an extraordinary achievement – he was a true Ferdinand Magellan of the wheel. Hundreds have followed his path since. But Stevens will always be the first, and remains unparalleled in his combination of adventurousness, humour and good old-fashioned pluck.

ACROSS ASIA BY BICYCLE
AMERICAN INNOCENTS ABROAD

The remarkable journey of Thomas Stevens soon encouraged other riders to follow in his path. In 1892, the 24-year-old Frank Lenz set out from Pittsburgh on a Victory Safety Bicycle to carry out his own circumnavigation. But after successfully crossing America, China, and India, Lenz's journey ended in tragedy. In May 1894 he disappeared on the road to Erzurum in Eastern Turkey, possibly drowned during a swollen river crossing, or more likely murdered by Kurdish brigands. Lenz's disappearance brought home the sober reality of late nineteenth-century travel to the East. The final photograph of him shows him astride his bike on a faraway Turkish road, peering wistfully into the lens from beneath a peaked cap.

Two other young Americans were more successful – Thomas Allen and William Sachtleben, graduates of the University of Washington. Sachtleben was the son of an Illinois businessman, known in his hometown for his athletic daring. At twenty-five he was two years older than Allen, an inch taller, and stronger. Allen, the son of a judge from St Louis, seemed less imposing, but was tenacious, and determined to follow his boyhood friend wherever destiny took them. At the heart of their plan was the impetuousness of youth, but also the brimming confidence of America in the late nineteenth century. Before long America would emerge from the First World War as a major world power, and Sachtleben and Allen's trip embodied this new Yankee confidence. Soon after graduating, they embarked on a cycling tour of England in 1890, riding Singer 'safeties', but soon asked themselves – why not keep going and take on Europe and Asia?

They upgraded their bicycles, procuring American-made Iroquois bikes with pneumatic tyres. They visited the American Ambassador (Abraham Lincoln's son), who asked if their parents knew what they were doing. Clearly these young men were seen as foolhardy, but Sachtleben defended their plan:

Traveling always by first class is like staying in your own country. There is such a thing as too much convenience. For our part, we have long since tired of trains and artificial, modern hotels. We love to roam on our bicycles, unfettered, among the scenes of unsophisticated nature and the common people.

Above Spik and Spanner. Allen and Sachtleben pose on their bikes in the safety of the photographic studio. Their custom-made bags are secured to their bicycle frames.

Messrs. Allen & Sachtleben. "Round the World" bicyclists.
Tu-yuen-Fu, Shansi, North China. Oct 18 1892   Chü-yüeh-wan.

They set off with specially designed bike packs, but with youthful impetuosity travelled without lights or brakes. They paid their respects to the explorers of the past, visiting the house of Christopher Columbus in Genoa. At other times they were less reverential - lapping Rome's Colosseum on their mounts.

As they passed into Asia their journey started proper. It was the area that Stevens had skirted around during his epic journey of 1884-6. They forsook the services of guides or interpreters, and decided to make their own way. In Sivas in central Turkey they both contracted typhoid, and relied on missionaries to nurse them back to health. For food, they had 'extraordinary dishes served to us, including daintily prepared leeches'. They climbed Mount Ararat, where Noah's Ark supposedly ran aground, standing at the intersection of Turkish, Russian and Persian empires. This part of the journey was an adventure in itself, as they spent the night sleeplessly at 11,000 feet, almost unable to eat because of their lack of saliva. Finally they made it to the domed summit, unfurling the Stars and Stripes and firing off their revolvers in celebration, although finding no signs of the Ark.

They continued their journey into Persia (Iran), demonstrating their bikes to the Governor at Meshed and meeting the Russian Consulate and his English wife. They visited the tomb of Tamburlaine at Samarkand in Uzbekistan. Sequestered over winter in Tashkent, Sachtleben nipped back to England for bicycle bits, travelling via Constantinople, arriving back in only 16 days. The two set off again in May, averaging seven miles an hour over the Russian steppes, before finally crossing the river Khorgos into China.

Above In China in October 1892, as they neared the end of their odyssey across Asia.

Right Tipping their hats to the locals, they take their leave of Tehran.

Delayed at customs while awaiting documentation, they set about learning Chinese. They shortened their handlebars and seat posts to save weight, and got a broken cog repaired by a blacksmith. China, isolated from the West, presented a new set of challenges. Their money and bills of credit were useless, and hordes surrounded them as they ate, mesmerised by the sight of these *yeh renn* or wild men with their long beards and their iron horses.

They traversed the great Gobi desert via a narrow fertile tract, eating homemade bread sweetened with sugar and fixing a broken frame with wire. Finally they reached the Western Gate of the Great Wall of China with telegraph lines overhead: civilization. They reached Beijing in early November 1892, spent the following month coasting through Japan, and then set sail for the States. They rode into New York in June 1893. Allen and Sachtleben had pedalled over 18,000 miles (28,968 km), but almost as importantly had taken thousands of pictures with their Eastman camera, and filled dozens of notebooks, with the publication of their exploits helping to propel the bike boom of the following years.

After an ill-fated expedition to discover the fate of his forerunner Frank Lenz, Sachtleben settled in Houston, and, by a strange coincidence, like Thomas Stevens became a theatrical manager. Thomas Allen, perhaps partly from the experience of spending two years patching together bicycles, became an engineer.

LEAVING TEHERAN FOR MESHED.

CYCLE TOURING
ON THE ROAD TO NOWHERE IN PARTICULAR

Late in the nineteenth century, following the adventures of figures like Thomas Stevens, bicycles came to be seen as more than eccentric entertainment but as a viable means of transport. And this interest soon evolved beyond transport into pleasure: the desire to see the world, to reconnect with nature and – in combination with that other late nineteenth-century invention, the photograph – to record it all and make one's own contribution to cycling history.

Right Totally lost. Cycle tourists consult the map on a country road somewhere in England in the 1930s.

Below A group of young American wheelmen pause to look at the Pacific on the Oregon coast highway in 1936.

The hobby of cycle touring thus grew up and soon became a favoured pastime among the middle classes. Writers, thinkers and musicians like Arthur Conan Doyle, George Bernard Shaw, Bertrand Russell, Thomas Hardy and Edward Elgar all pedalled their way across the English countryside. H.G. Wells summed up the this free-wheeling optimism: 'When I see an adult on a bicycle, I do not despair for the future of the human race.'

In 1896, the Cycle Touring Club was formed in England, and by 1899 it had amassed 60,000 members. It organised rallies, produced guides and campaigned for its members, opening Regent's Park and Richmond Park to cyclists. It placed warning signs at the top of steep hills. Its members often rode in uniform so that they might recognise fellow members. In America, The League of American Wheelmen was founded in 1880; by 1898, it had more than 100,000 avid cyclists. The French followed soon after with the Fédération Française de Cyclotourisme. The French novelist Emile Zola was a keen cyclist, and in his novel *Paris* (1898), recorded the thrill of a bicycling excursion:

> *The two let their machines carry them down the hill. And then this happy rush of speed overtook them, the dizzying sense of balance in the lightning-like, breathtaking descent on wheels, while the grey path flew beneath their feet and the trees whisked past at either side like the slat of a fan as it unfolds... That is the endless hope, the liberation from the all too oppressive fetters, across space. And no exultation is better, hearts leap under the open sky.*

What was particularly important in England, and subsequently across much of Europe, was the introduction of a 40-hour working week with two weeks' paid holiday per year. Now working men and women were blessed with a certain degree of leisure time and holiday time, but in an age before cheap jet travel, required an economic means of getting away. The bicycle offered this economic freedom, and also provided a dramatic contrast for many people's workaday, industrialised week. In *The Wheels of Chance*, H.G. Wells captures this new-found freedom in the figure of Hoopdriver, a frustrated draper who is liberated by his wheeling machine:

> *Only those who toil six long days out of the seven, and all the year round, save for one brief glorious fortnight or ten days in the summer time, know the exquisite sensations of the First Holiday Morning. All the dreary, uninteresting routine drops from you suddenly, your chains fall about your feet [...] There were thrushes in the Richmond Road, and a lark on Putney Heath. The freshness of dew was in the air; dew or the relics of an overnight shower glittered on the leaves and grass [...] He wheeled his machine up Putney Hill, and his heart sang within him.*

An image from *Picture Post* in 1939: keen cycle tourists heading into the hills in 1939. A milk delivery boy looks enviously on.

Hang Hiking! Oh for a
Hercules

With the advent of the car in the twentieth century, the middle classes soon moved on to more cosseted forms of travel. But cycle touring remained the favoured occupation of the lower-middle and working classes. The Cycle Touring Club organised week-long tours, with stays at recommended hotels, for as little as £3 and 10s. Camping equipment, once demobbed military equipment, was now designed for lightness and ease of use. County Guides were published, guiding riders to the most scenic routes and affordable hotels.

What was key for many was the sympathy between cycle touring and the 'Outdoor' movement of the interwar period. In Germany, youth hostelling was invented, aimed at encouraging international cooperation and understanding in the aftermath of the war. England soon followed suit with the Youth Hostel Association being formed in 1930; by 1939, it had 297 hostels and 83,000 members. Cycle touring thus became an essential part of the English holiday landscape, immortalised in the works of Enid Blyton, whose *Famous Five* books captured a childhood idyll of Timmy the dog, picnics, ginger beer, bicycle pumps and cycling.

MODERN BIKES FOR CYCLE TOURING

Specialist bikes are available, often starting at around £500, featuring a steel rather than aluminium frame (steel offers a more forgiving ride). But a bike need not be new or expensive: any decent bike will do if it is properly prepared. But a key question is whether to choose a bike with 700c wheels (the typical wheel on a road or touring bike), or 26-inch wheels, typical of a mountain bike. If you are thinking of riding in the developing world or often on unpaved roads, then 26-inch is the sensible choice: they are stronger and spares are easily available. If you are riding good roads with bike shops easily accessible, 700c will giving you a little less rolling resistance (about 10%), as the contact point is longer and narrower, although the difference is easily overstated; the quality of the rims and tyres are of equal importance.

THE ART OF THE BICYCLE

By the last decade of the nineteenth century there were around a million bicycles in Europe – most of them in Britain, but many in France, Germany and Belgium. The bike therefore flourished during one of the most important periods in modern history – when the women's movement gained ground, when Marconi invented the radio and at the height of the European powers' 'scramble for Africa' and the tensions that would lead to the First World War. But it was also a period of great artistic innovation.

Impressionists and post-Impressionists reacted against the static realistic mode of nineteenth-century art and started to experiment with new techniques and ideas – a more dynamic sense of the instability of reality and the active role of perception. But what was crucial to this new aesthetic was a sense of movement, and of speed, reflecting the new realities of an industrialised world. And bicycles came to be seen as a suitable subject of the artist's muse – symbolising the haste and excitement of modernity.

Left Henri de Toulouse-Lautrec: La Chaîne Simpson advertising poster from 1896.

Right Impressionist Georges Stein's *The Champs-Elysées*.

Certainly bicycles had been depicted by traditional painters. One spurious myth that gained ground in the early twentieth century was that Leonardo had scribbled a bicycle design on the back of one of his codexes, although this has now been shown to be a complete myth. But the bicycle boom of the 1890s coincided with the great age of French poster art. With the rise of capitalism and industrialisation, art itself became 'commodified' – advertising rose to new heights of artistry and expertise. (see page 110), and the bicycle became the apple in the eye of this new commercial style. For a new generation of art nouveau artists and designers, the curves and circles of the bicycle became almost a mirror image of the human form. Inevitably the posters combined bicycles with beautiful women – perhaps reflecting new female freedoms – but also reflecting a sense that the curves of the bicycle were implicitly feminine.

This sense of the gracefulness of the bicycle can be seen in the Impressionist female artist Georges Stein's painting of the Champs-Elysées. Stein specialised in scenes of city life, drawn to the shifting kaleidoscope of the ever-expanding capital. The busyness of the city can be seen here: the road crowded with carriages, dogs and soldiers on horseback; a man with a stick attempting to cross; it has recently rained – the road reflects the light and the trees – but is clearing now, with the clouds disappearing to the left, and the sun coming out. The road appears to be living up to its reputation as the 'Elysian Fields' – a classical paradise - or as the Parisians have it: 'la plus belle avenue du monde'.

Speed and Power –
Umberto Boccioni's
*Dynamism
of a Cyclist*, 1913.

But our perspective is that of the young female cyclist who is nimbly negotiating the puddled road, standing on her pedals. She is going against the flow it seems, with the horses and carriages riding towards her. A mounted soldier shoots her an admiring glance, as does his horse at her bike. But she appears oblivious, her path squarely aimed at the Arc de Triomphe in the distance. She represents a fresh new wave of Frenchness, as opposed to the weight of history surrounding her: fashionable, free-wheeling, light on her feet.

One of the most important artists to discover the aesthetic attractions of the bicycle was the post-Impressionist painter Henri de Toulouse-Lautrec. A childhood accident had left him with shortened legs, and as a result he was unable to ride, but he became an avid fan of cycling, befriending the editor of *Le Journal des Velocipedistes* and attending local races. According to his biographer, Frey, he watched cycle racing, and the society that surrounded it, 'with the same intensity that he watched a line of dancers or a circus bareback rider, attracted by the beauty of movement, but also by the smells, sounds and excitement of the spectacle'.

A lasting testament to Toulouse-Lautrec's interest is the cycle poster he designed for the English chain manufacturer Simpson. It shows the top racer, Constant Huret, on a bike with a 'Simpson lever chain' (which was supposed to improve efficiency) about to overtake a pair of riders on a tandem. Simpson chains, it seems, give one man the power of many. Toulouse-Lautrec's depiction is accurate and informative – as all posters need to be – but deftly also suggests the excitement of the bicycle: the sleek blues of the riders, the society figures eagerly spectating and the tightly drawn leg muscles whirling around. For those wanting a Simpson chain, the local supplier is also noted – appropriately enough, a monsieur L.B. Spoke, at 25 Boulevard Haussmann.

The bicycle also found a home in the Futurist movement of the early twentieth century. In 1909, F.T. Marinetti published the 'Futurist Manifesto', declaring: 'Time and space died yesterday' and that 'We affirm that the world's magnificence has been enriched by a new beauty: the beauty of speed'. Bicycles, more than any other invention, seemed to embody the Futurist dream of a merging of the human and the mechanical, as can be seen in Umberto Boccioni's *Dynamism of a Cyclist* (1913). Developed from a series of increasingly abstract sketches, the painting shows a racing cyclist and his machine becoming at one with the speed with which they are travelling. The canvas is a vortex of cones and curves and 'lines of force' – the almost cartoonish Futurist way of celebrating movement. A red and orange track seems to curve away to the left, and a hilly landscape can be seen on the right. But all the viewer's attention is centred on the rider, created from blues and browns, a mixture of mechanism and muscle. Here the bicycle is not a vehicle, a means of getting somewhere, but an experience in itself, a challenge to pedestrian views of reality and a celebration of the Futurists' 'beauty of speed'.

MORE NOTABLE BICYCLES IN ART

Pablo Picasso, *Bull's Head* (1942) – perhaps the most simple but powerful bicycling modern artwork: a saddle and a pair of handlebars joined together to make a bull.

Jean Metzinger's *At the Cycle-Race Track* (*Au vélodrome*, 1912), an important Cubist artist goes to the races.

Marcel Duchamp, *Bicycle Wheel* (1913) – one of Duchamp's 'readymades' – here a bicycle wheel and forks attached to a kitchen stool.

Mario Sironi's *The Cyclist* (*Il ciclista*, 1916) another Italian futurist celebration of muscularity and speed.

ON THE ROAD AND OFF

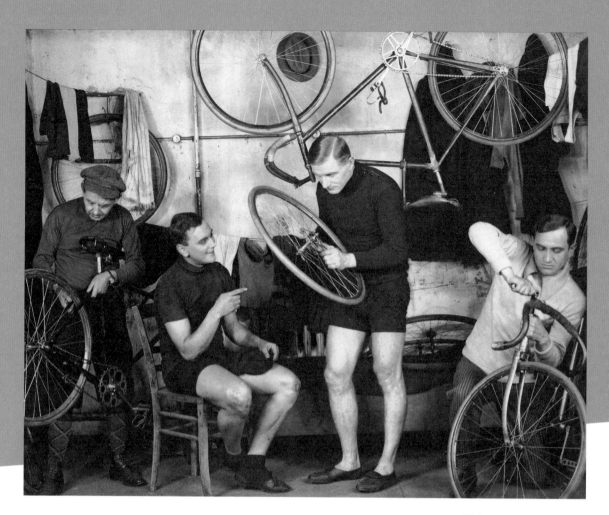

Maintenance is an ongoing process and can be performed in a variety of workwear.

BASIC MAINTENANCE

Look after your bike and your bike will look after you. It sounds a little trite but it is so true. At its most basic, and even at its more complex, the bike is a pretty simple machine, but if you don't look after it properly you will very quickly get into problems. The adage 'little and often' is very apt here because a lot of what follows doesn't take long but you need to do some of it before every journey.

Equipment

FOOT PUMP This is probably the most essential piece of maintenance kit so it's worth investing in a good one. The hand-pumps that most off-the-shelf bikes come with are fine for putting air into the tubes after a puncture fix, but you really need a foot pump to put proper pressure in.

OLD TOOTHBRUSHES They say you should change your toothbrush every three or four months and that's good news for your bike maintenance. There's almost nothing better for getting into those tight areas when cleaning.

ALLEN KEY A good set of allen keys is vital, and not just for fixing your Ikea furniture. Most nuts and bolts on bikes now need William G. Allen's invention (originally called the hex key).

WORKSTAND If you really want to go to town, get yourself a workstand. Say goodbye to the days of trying to clean your bike while it sits upside down, or leant up against the wall.

CLEANERS There's a big market in different types of cleaning fluids so shop around. The desire to go green has meant that this end of the market is very well served.

CHAIN CLEANING KIT This can be a useful and efficient time saver. In effect it gives your chain a scrub and bath all in one go without having to take it off the bike.

Before Every Journey

TYRES A squeeze will tell you if the pressure is right but it is worth giving the tyres some air every couple of days. This is important not just to make the ride easier and more comfortable, but it also helps prevent punctures. A properly pressurised tyre reduces the chances both of impact punctures and foreign body punctures. It's also worth giving the surface of the tyre a quick check to make sure it hasn't picked anything up that might be pushed through.

LIGHTS Turn them on before leaving home just to make sure they're working, even if you think you'll be home before dark.

Weekly

BRAKES Engage brakes, make sure they are contacting the rim properly and that the pads aren't worn.

CHAIN Give it a quick look to check it is lubricated.

WHEELS Give them a spin to make sure they are running true. Even a slight jiggle could lead to major problems.

Monthly

ALL MOVING PARTS Give them a proper clean with brushes and cloths. Re-lubricate where appropriate. The cleaning is vital on the chain and cogs; any grit that gets left in there for too long will soon become a grinding paste that wears away the edges of everything it touches.

BOLTS AND SCREWS Make sure they're all tight. These things work loose over time and before you know it they've fallen off.

BRAKE AND GEAR CABLES Make sure the tension is right, and there's no rust build up or wear.

SPOKES Tighten any that are loose, replace any that are bent.

Bike workshops the world over know the benefits of regular maintenance and properly inflated tyres.

Six monthly

- Give everything a really thorough clean. Having done everything above this will not be as arduous as it could be, but make this one a really proper valet, including the frame, the rims, the mud-guards. Imagine you're entering a 'best-looking bike' competition the next day so that you don't scrimp.

- This is also a good time to give your puncture repair kit the once-over just to make sure it's fully stocked and ready for action.

- Once a year you'll probably want to replace the tape on your handlebars. You'd be surprised how dirty it gets.

BMX BANDITRY

BMX, or to use its full title Bicycle Motocross, is the naughty cousin of traditional cycling competition that, to the surprise of many, even gained Olympic status at the 2008 Beijing Games. In just 40 years it had come a long way from the dirt trails of Southern California to the top table of world sport but, like any BMX course, the journey was not without its lumps, bumps and falls.

It is generally accepted that the sport was born in California but there is evidence to show that it was actually in the flatlands of the Netherlands that it was first competed. The cover of the Dutch magazine *Ach Lieve Tijd* (Oh Dear Time) from 1956 shows a couple of young boys racing on a dirt track on adapted short-framed bikes. The discovery of this information altered the timeline of BMX history but has been glossed over by many as an anomaly, as the sport didn't take off and no formal organisation was started at that time.

The Oscar-nominated documentary *On Any Sunday* was ostensibly a film about motorcycles, but it proved pivotal for the spread of BMX.

Back on the accepted historical timeline the vital catalyst was the introduction of the Schwinn Stingray in 1963. As the Schwinn advert originally claimed, it is known as the 'bike that changed cycling'. Its radical design was based on what kids in Southern California were already doing to their bikes, by replacing the factory supplied saddles and handlebars with those mimicking the easy-rider style of the motorbike. Al Fritz's design with the long, low-hung seat, the high handlebars and 20-inch wheels, marked the Stingray out as a market leader even though Schwinn's management had initially been sceptical. It caught the imagination and the forward thinking feel of the sixties, selling over 45,000 in just the first few months.

If the Stingray sowed the seeds and kids' enthusiastic take-up and imaginative uses of the bike were what nourished it in its infancy, then it has to be a short segment in the opening credits of the film *On Any Sunday* that ultimately brought BMX screaming and kicking into the wider world. After a few shots of adults on motorbikes the opening credits are shown over a series of shots of kids, aged around 10 or 11, racing around improvised dirt tracks. They go over jumps, do tricks and finally we are treated to one of the gang performing an extended wheelie down the street.

While BMX as an informal hobby had already gained a strong foothold in Southern California, it was this ninety seconds of footage that catapulted it to national prominence and beyond. Within three years George E. Esser had set up the National Bicycle League (NBL). His two sons raced motorcycles and had also started racing BMX, but found there was no formal organisation arranging competitions. Dad stepped up to the plate. The NBL was followed and, in some respects superseded, by the American Bicycle Association (ABA) in 1977.

The ABA quickly became the official organisation for BMX competitions, putting on events and running tracks up and down the country. It currently sanctions over 10,000 races a year and runs nearly 400 tracks. As in other sports, such as boxing, there has been a certain amount of jockeying for position and splintering whereby other organisations have set up as sanctioning bodies. These have included the National Bicycle League,

Image from a Schwinn pamphlet of kids riding their Stingray bikes in Griffith Park, Los Angeles, around 1972.

National Bicycle Association, National Pedal Sport Association and United Bicycle Racers Association, but it is the ABA that has outlasted them all.

The sport's growth continued around the globe and 1981 saw the founding of the International BMX Federation (IBF). It had been three years earlier that the first *unofficial* world championship had been held. This was organised by promoter and Hollywood actor Renny Roker and his JAG BMX organisation. The first five World Championships were organised by JAG BMX before the IBF took over, and the first JAG BMX World Champion was Stu Thomsen.

With the increase in well-organised competitions and great leaps and bounds forward in the number of competitors worldwide, it was not long before BMX was taken under the wing of the mainstream cycling's world body the UCI – Union Cycliste International – in 1993. This stamp of approval from the formal wing of the sport meant there was only one final hurdle to be leapt for BMX to join the established sporting world, and in 2008 it made that jump, literally as we'll see, when it became one of the sports at the Beijing Olympic Games.

So that's the journey of the sport, but what is the sport itself? Those early pioneers raced and tricked their way around improvised homemade courses, doing wheelies and leaps just for the sheer joy of it, but how has that been formalised into a competitive sport? There are two branches of competition, which can be traced back to the early days, namely racing and doing tricks. These are described formally as BMX Supercross and BMX Freestyle. It is the former that is competed for at the Olympics.

BMX Supercross is a straight race with the first rider across the line winning, but there is nothing straight about the course. A lot is packed into a course length of just 350* metres. There are tight banked 180-degree turns, jumps and flat sections on a track which is just ten metres wide, along which eight riders compete. The basic elements of all courses are the same, with three corners and four straights, but a lot can happen between the start and the finish.

Races at the elite level start at the top of an eight-metre high ramp so that the riders can quickly build up speed for the race. It is the jump sections that really make this sport so exciting, especially as there is not just one type of jump, so the rider's ability and nerve are tested to the limit. There are six main types of jump:

DOUBLE Two jumps close together where the quickest way across is to jump the gap between them.

STEP-UP A short hill, closely followed by a bigger one.

STEP-DOWN The opposite of the Step-Up.

Taking flight looks spectacular but if you do it at the wrong moment you lose time, so the rider has to make quick choices based on where the other riders are and what hills, jumps or corners are coming up. It's a helter-skelter rollercoaster of a race and gets the pulse of the crowd racing as much as that of the riders. The beauty of the sport is that, due to the shape of the course, it can be fitted into quite a small area and is easy for a big crowd to enjoy. (*Courses can be anywhere between 300 and 400 metres, but 350 is the Olympic distance.)

BMX Freestyle, as the name suggests, is much more freeform and is not a race but more of an artistic endeavour. There are no rules, as such, for freestyle. Points are awarded based on how difficult a jump or figure is, its originality and the style or panache with which it was performed. Freestyle events or courses are split into five main categories:

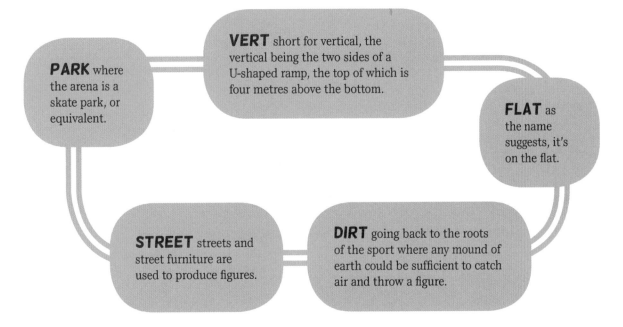

PARK where the arena is a skate park, or equivalent.

VERT short for vertical, the vertical being the two sides of a U-shaped ramp, the top of which is four metres above the bottom.

FLAT as the name suggests, it's on the flat.

STREET streets and street furniture are used to produce figures.

DIRT going back to the roots of the sport where any mound of earth could be sufficient to catch air and throw a figure.

The amazing thing about BMX is that in spite of its journey from the dirt trails of Southern California to becoming a global sport, it has not lost the spirit of those early days. It continues to provide thrills and spills without the cynicism that is often associated with other professional sports.

ROLLER
A small hill on its own or in combination with others.

TABLE TOP
A jump with a flat top.

RHYTHM SECTION A group of hills all together where the rider must decide whether catching air or staying on the track is the quickest route through.

This is just a training session! Some of the world's best preparing for the 2015 UCI BMX World Championship in Zolder, Belgium.

FIRST OLYMPIC GOLD MEDALLISTS

MEN
Māris Štrombergs
of Latvia

WOMEN
Anne-Caroline
Chausson
of France

THE BICYCLE IN FILM

**The bicycle and the cinema grew up together. The first Safety Bicycle –
featuring a diamond frame and chain drive – was invented in 1885. The
first moving picture – 'Sortie de l'usine Lumière de Lyon' – was made by
the Lumière brothers soon after in 1894. It shows workers leaving the
Lumière photographic factory and alongside dogs, horses and carriages,
features no fewer than three bikes: one pushed by a man in a straw boater,
the other two pedalling away from the crowd – no doubt the first to arrive
home after a hard day's work.**

Film is about movement, and bikes are about
movement too. It is therefore not surprising that
the film industry has had a lifelong love affair with
the bike. From the Lumière brothers to Tim Burton,
the bicycle has symbolised the hopes, dreams and
disillusionments of twentieth-century life.

Perhaps the most famous of all bicycle films is
Vittorio de Sica's *Bicycle Thieves* (1948). It tells the
story of a poor billposter, Antonio Ricci, who scours
Rome looking for his bicycle after it is stolen as he
is pasting up a poster of the American film star Rita
Hayworth. The film thus juxtaposes the dreams
of a postwar world and the impoverishment of life
in a defeated Italy. Significantly, the brand of the
bicycle that is stolen is 'Fides' – meaning faith. De
Sica cast non-actors in the main roles, and at first
it was received unfavourably in Italy for its negative
portrayal of Italian life. But for its realism and
humanity, it is now seen as one of the greatest films
of all time.

The link between bicycles and work is also an
ingredient in Jacques Tati's *Jour de Fête* ('The Big
Day') (1949). But whereas de Sica's film was about
loss, Tati's comedy, starring himself as François
the hyperactive postman, captured the exuberance
and joie de vivre of the bike. After drinking too
much during the village fête, and watching a
newsreel of the U.S. postal service dropping mail

from helicopters, François decides to speed up his rounds. What follows is a masterpiece of film art and stunt choreography, as he takes on cars, animals, hosepipes and, finally - in this satire of technological innovation — his own runaway bike.

The emotional intimacy between French cinema and French cycling can also be also in the animated film *Belleville Rendez-vous* (2003) (*Les Triplettes de Belleville*), directed by Sylvain Chomet and nominated for two Oscars. It tells the story of an old woman, Madame Souza, and her grandson, Champion. There's very little speaking in this odd, touchingly funny and charming film, which tells its story through images, pantomime and song. Grandmother Souza is growing worried about Champion, who after the loss of his parents, seems to be becoming more lugubriously melancholic every day. She offers him piano lessons. She buys him a puppy. But finally, leafing through his scrapbook she discovers his love of cycling — his parents were cyclists — and encourages him in his dream of winning the Tour de France. An intensive Grandma-directed training regime ensues that sees her massaging his aching calves with a hoover. But while out racing Champion is kidnapped by the mafia. His rescue requires the combined efforts of Grandma Souza, Bruno the dog and a song and dance trio called the Belleville Sisters, whom Champion used to watch on the telly as a kid. This wonderful work of art is a wistful celebration of Frenchness - paying honour to Jacques Tati, and the jazz guitarist Django Reinhardt - but it also captures the French love of the bike. As the film unfolds, Madame Souza's house becomes cluttered with the paraphernalia of cycling: some trophies, old bike bits and clothing, a broken derailleur; it even sports a bicycle weather vane.

Left *Jour de Fête*, 1949, a classic French comedy about a hyperactive postman.

Above Another French film, *Belleville Rendez-vous* (2003), with cycling at its core.

There are therefore films about bikes. But there are of course many more films with bikes in them. One of the earliest, and most famous scenes involving a bike, is *The Wizard of Oz* (1939). Miss Gulch, the nasty bicycling neighbour of Dorothy (Judy Garland), threatens to have her dog, Toto, put down. During a storm, Dorothy is hit on the head by a window frame and sees Miss Gulch transformed into a witch, her bike morphing into a broomstick as she cycles through the air. In other films the bike is the hero. In Steven Spielberg's *E.T.* (1982) the local BMX bandits get together to help Elliott smuggle E.T. out of town. A thrilling pursuit follows, with BMXers flummoxing the forces of adulthood with their off-road skills. But as they approach a final cordon of police cars, Elliott closes his eyes and the boys — and their bikes — take off. It's *Close Encounters* meets *Home Alone* meets *Peter Pan*.

Other famous bicycling scenes are more romantic. In *Butch Cassidy and the Sundance Kid* (1969) the bicycle becomes a form of foreplay, with the schoolmarm Etta (Katherine Ross) decorously poised on Paul Newman's handlebars as they take a ride on a summer's day. He courts her with a display of trick cycling: standing on the saddle; riding backwards; goofing around; until he finally crashes backwards through a fence, watched piteously by a long-horned bull. The crash, like the bicycle, is a symbol of modernity in this romance of American innocence, horses and the Wild West. As Newman goes on the run he throws the bike aside, saying: 'The future's yours, you lousy bicycle.'

TOP BICYCLE FILMS

BOY AND BICYCLE
(1965)

A boy plays truant

A SUNDAY IN HELL
(1976)

Documentary following the 1976 Paris-Roubaix race

BREAKING AWAY
(1979)

Coming of age in the States

Left Paul Newman woos Etta with his trick cycling in the classic *Butch Cassidy and the Sundance Kid*, 1969.

Below A still from *Jour de Fête*, 1949.

But perhaps the film that best captures the perpetual childhood of bicycle-love is *Pee-wee's Big Adventure* (1985) starring Paul Reubens and directed by Tim Burton. In an absurdist twist on *Bicycle Thieves*, the story tells how Pee-wee's souped-up Schwinn is stolen while he is in the mall. Despite his offer of a $10,000 dollar reward, a chase across the States ensues, with Pee-wee befriending a gang of Hell's Angels and hitching a ride with a ghostly trucker named 'Large Marge' on the way. In a final post-modern twist, Pee-wee learns that his bike has become a prop in a film, and is himself cast in a Ninja movie as a bellboy. It's unashamedly infantile but loads of fun. The opening shot shows Pee-wee cruising effortlessly past a peloton of professional racing cyclists (it's all a dream). Yet ultimately truth is stranger – or more bike-obsessed – than fiction: in 2015 the Schwinn from the film sold on Ebay for $36,000.

BMX BANDITS

(1983)

Kids turn bicycle detectives

THE FLYING SCOTSMAN

(2006)

Biopic of Scottish champion Graeme Obree

BELLEVILLE RENDEZ-VOUS

(2003)

Enchanting animated tale of a boy racer and his grandmother

THE BIRTH OF THE

It's somewhat of a misnomer to call these chunky-wheeled cycles mountain bikes because they don't really go up and down the likes of Everest. A more accurate name would be 'off-roader' as this is how they are generally used, and why they were first created way back at the tail end of the nineteenth century.

MOUNTAIN BIKE

It was in May 1896 that 2nd Lieutenant James A. Moss was given permission to put together the 25th Infantry Bicycle Corps. A keen cyclist, Moss co-designed these hardy bikes with the A.G. Spalding Company. These first off-roaders had steel rims, tandem spokes and extra-heavy side forks and crowns. To the naked eye they didn't look so different from a standard road bike but they weighed a hefty 32 pounds, which went up to 59 when fully laden.

Moss, a graduate of West Point, was originally from Louisiana, and as soon as he got hold of his bikes he started putting his corps through their paces, or rather pedals! The training was necessary to prepare his men, a team of eight enlisted soldiers, for an 800-mile expedition from Fort Missoula in Montana to Yellowstone Park in Wyoming – and back again. After leaving camp on 15 August it took the corps ten days to make the outward half of the trip, arriving on 24 August 1896. It was considered enough of a success to take the plunge and take a larger group on a longer, more gruelling trip to fully test the concept.

The second great military cycling expedition would take 20 men on a 1,900-mile journey to St Louis in Missouri. It was such big news that a reporter, Edward Boos, came along to send daily reports to the newspapers in the towns at either end of the route. Rations were carried for two days with re-supplies arranged at 100-mile intervals along the route. This longer trip really did put the bikes and their riders through all possible trials. Moss recorded that over the 34 days of travel, 13 hours were lost repairing the bikes, over four hours fixing punctures with 117 hours spent taking lunch and 71 hours lost for 'other reasons'. We can only guess what those other reasons were but saddle soreness was probably near the top of the list.

The journey took 34 days at an average of just under 56 miles a day at a speed of 6.3 miles per hour. It doesn't take a brilliant mathematician to see that this meant spending nearly 9 hours a day in the saddle (although it was reported that some of the terrain was so bad that it was necessary to get off and push on occasion). Maybe that's where the phrase push-bike comes from.

The 25th Infantry Bicycle Corps pose with their bikes at Minerva Terrace, Yellowstone National Park, in 1896.

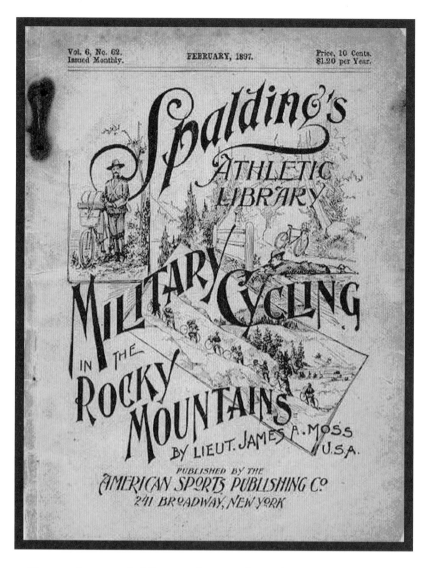

These early mountain bikes are a long way from what we now understand by the name, but the longest journey starts with the first step and so everyone who has ever careered down a hillside has to take their cycle helmet off in a moment of thanks to the visionary that was Lieutenant Moss.

Lt Moss would probably be surprised and delighted in equal measure with the way mountain biking and the machines used for it have developed since his first efforts. For him and his men these bikes were a practical necessity to get their work done but now they are almost exclusively leisure or sporting machines.

The early development of off-road cycling as a sport, be it mountain biking or its close cousin cyclo-cross, can be traced back to the cyclists who used it as

1896
MOSS'S CYCLE CORPS 6.3 MPH

a method of training for their on-road competitions. By cycling away from the tarmac, competitors improved their handling skills, increased their fitness levels and gave them a break from the drudgery of the tarmac-bashing that on-road training could easily become. In spite of all this time spent cycling off-road it wasn't until the 1960s that genuinely specialist bikes began to appear for the purpose.

As with much innovation in cycling, the drive for new machines began with enthusiasts making their own adjustments and modifications to off-the-shelf products. Cruiser bikes like those made by Schwinn were some of the first to be 'pimped' in this way. With their heavy frames and wider tyres these were perfect for the rough and ready unpredictable terrain. Riders of these called them 'klunkers', a term arrived at by onomatopoeia thanks to the battering the rider took.

The actual name 'mountain bike' could have come from several sources but most people are happy to credit Joe Breeze. He is certainly recognised as the person to design, from scratch, the first bike specifically for mountain biking. He built his first 'Breezer' in 1978 for his own use in off-road races. It won first time out and thus the trail was set and his design can be seen in the mountain bikes still used today.

2015
ERIC BARONE 138.75 MPH

ALL DOWNHILL FROM HERE

Sometime in the early 1970s a group of hippies discovered a fire road flanking the southern side of Pine Mountain in Northern California. It was traditionally a haven for hikers and fishermen – offering uninterrupted views of the Bay and some of the best trout fishing in the area. Yet fuelled by the counter-culture of west coast America, this band of modern discoverers decided to do something different: ride the downhill trail on bikes. But rather than using traditional road bikes, with narrow tyres and handlebars, they turned to 1940s Schwinn Excelsior balloon-tyred bikes – the traditional, leisurely ride of the American paperboy, whose wide handlebars allowed him to fling papers over fences without losing control. But here the wide bars served a different purpose – allowing unhelmeted riders, hurtling down a bumpy rocky track, to stay onboard, with the wide tyres to some extent softening the ride.

PINE MOUNTAIN TRAIL

At this particular moment in the early seventies, two things were therefore born – the 'klunker', the modified Schwinn bicycle that was the first incarnation of the mountain bike; and the sport of downhill racing, which in recent years has been proposed as the next Winter Olympic sport (cross country mountain biking already featuring in the Olympics since 1996).

As the reputation of the Pine Mountain trail grew, more competitive riders arrived from local cycle clubs, such as the Velo Club Tamalpais a few miles away. Bikes were modified: derailleur gears were added; frames were given added strengthening. 'Cascade Canyon Road' even gained a new name – 'Repack Road', as a result of the old hub brakes overheating and needing to be repacked with grease.

The start line was on a ridge at the top of Pine Mountain, and the first timed race was on 21 October 1976, and was won by Bob Burrowes. The fastest time was set by Gary Fisher at 4:22 for the 2-mile course (Fisher was to go on to become a well-known mountain bike designer). The riders set off at two-minute intervals with faster riders setting off behind slower ones – which increased the finish line excitement and drama.

Soon word began to spread. 'California bikies are mountainside surfing' ran a headline in *VeloNews* in February 1978. The local TV company came and filmed a segment for their evening news show. Soon other frame-builders and manufacturers caught the off-road craze. The first mass-produced bike was the Specialized Stumpjumper, which came out in 1981. It had a steel frame, a modified BMX stem, and motorcycle-style handlebars, and sold for $750. But key to the success of downhill mountain biking as a sport was the invention of suspension – avoided on road bikes because of the extra weight – but essential if one was to travel off road downhill at speed. RockShox produced the RS-1 front suspension forks in 1989, by simply adapting

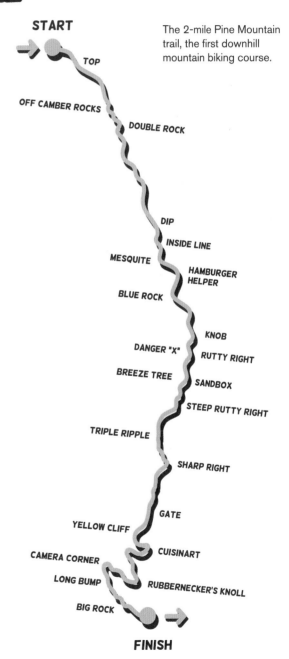

The 2-mile Pine Mountain trail, the first downhill mountain biking course.

START
TOP
OFF CAMBER ROCKS
DOUBLE ROCK
DIP
INSIDE LINE
MESQUITE
HAMBURGER HELPER
BLUE ROCK
KNOB
DANGER "X"
RUTTY RIGHT
BREEZE TREE
SANDBOX
STEEP RUTTY RIGHT
TRIPLE RIPPLE
SHARP RIGHT
GATE
YELLOW CLIFF
CUISINART
CAMERA CORNER
LONG BUMP
RUBBERNECKER'S KNOLL
BIG ROCK
FINISH

Left Pioneering mountain bikers in the 1970s, ready to take on the Pine Mountain trail in Northern California.

Above Argentina's Pablo Seawald lifts off in the final of the Valparaíso Downhill of 2012.

Right Coby Jordan approaching the Repack finish line in 1976.

motorcycle technology, and the first full-suspension mountain bike, the Gary Fisher RS-1, followed in 1992.

Fast forward forty years and downhill mountain bike racing is now an established sport. The bikes have developed to deal with much longer and more arduous descents. Unlike the Californian klunkers, they have suspension front and rear, usually with 7-10 inches of travel. The frames are stronger than traditional cross-country mountain bikes, and are designed to have a slacker steering head angle to increase stability, and a longer wheelbase than traditional mountain bikes. Powerful disc brakes both slow the bike, but also help dissipate the heat created by the friction.

In terms of technique, riders need to harness the natural momentum provided by gravity, and travel from the top of the course to the bottom in the fastest possible time. In this sense balance, muscle stamina and courage are far more important than the athleticism required in other cycling sports. And crashes are frequent. Riders need to wear a full-face helmet rather than simply a cycling helmet, goggles to protect against not only dust but also branches and other large debris, and body armour is a good idea – elbow and knee protectors and possibly a neck support. As always, getting back to nature safely in terms of downhill mountain biking requires a certain degree of investment. Following a spate of accidents and collisions, the trails around Pine Mountain now have a speed limit of 15 miles an hour. At the height of the mountain bike craze the police took to using radar speed guns to trap speeding riders.

But in a final irony, downhill mountain biking has also gone urban. One of the most famous courses is in the Chilean seaport of Valparaíso, what is often

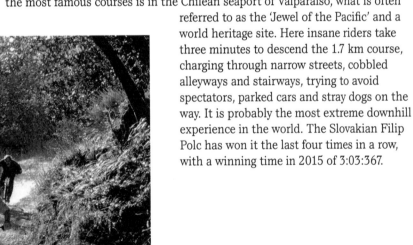

referred to as the 'Jewel of the Pacific' and a world heritage site. Here insane riders take three minutes to descend the 1.7 km course, charging through narrow streets, cobbled alleyways and stairways, trying to avoid spectators, parked cars and stray dogs on the way. It is probably the most extreme downhill experience in the world. The Slovakian Filip Polc has won it the last four times in a row, with a winning time in 2015 of 3:03:367.

ICONIC BIKES

The Schwinn Cruiser

Arnold, Schwinn and Company was formed in Chicago during the peak of the worldwide bicycle boom in 1895. It was the brainchild of the German-born Ignaz Schwinn, who had emigrated to America in 1891. By 1916 the company had produced one million bicycles, often for other retailers, such as Sears, to rebadge under their own name. But with the coming of the motor car and the motorcycle and the Great Depression of the 1930s, bicycle sales fell. Moreover, Schwinn, heavily exposed to falling stocks and shares, lost a fortune, and left the company.

His son, Frank Schwinn, took over and made the company refocus on bicycles, filing patents for a number of innovations including sprung front forks and a cantilevered frame. But his most important innovation was the introduction of low-pressure balloon tyres, after seeing their popularity on the cobbled roads of Germany. In 1933, a newly designed bike, the B10-E was marketed, looking like a motorbike with imitation fuel tank (a tool box), a rear carrier, a Klaxon horn and a chromed motorcycle-style head light. Many bike shops were unenthusiastic, but the public was sold on the idea. In the first year of the new design, 100,000 bikes were sold, and three years later they were selling 200,000 annually.

Key to Schwinn's success were things like lifetime frame guarantees (they calculated that if a frame was to fail it would be in the first year, so the risk was minimal). But the design also appealed to youngsters, not old enough for, or able to afford, a motorbike. In 1934 they introduced the Schwinn Aerocycle, with sprung seat and aeroplane design on the 'fuel tank'. It was an instant hit. The following years saw Schwinn innovate on the basic design, giving bikes such names as 'Phantom', 'Hornet' and 'Panther', featuring such goodies as twin headlights, monogrammed seat and electric horns.

The Schwinn became one of the iconic images of America through the 1940s right through to the 1950s, and the best-selling bike of the century. With their strength and cushioned ride they became perfect paperboy bikes, Schwinn even designing a 'Wasp' model for the job, with heavier spokes and double rear baskets. They were an embodiment of the American Dream itself, glamorous, but hardworking; extravagant yet reliable; tough, but fun.

The Raleigh 3-Speed Roadster

The Raleigh 3-Speed Roadster is as English as Yorkshire pudding, fish and chips and Rule Britannia. First designed in the 1930s, the design remained pretty much the same throughout the rest of the century, offering comfort, reliability and a certain understated English style.

Raleigh was formed by Sir Frank Bowden in 1890, taking its name from the street in Nottingham on which the factory was situated, the street itself taking its name from one of England's greatest heroes. The following years saw the company grow, and in 1893 it won its first world sprint and 10km championship with the American A.A. 'Zimmy' Zimmerman.

At this point in time, Raleigh made bikes very much like many other English safety bike manufacturers, such as Hercules and BSA. But in 1901, Raleigh engineers were inspired by patents awarded to Henry Sturmey and James Archer for a three-speed geared rear hub. Bowden bought up the designs, before settling on Archer's (although originally designed by William Reilly). In 1903, the geared hub saw the light of day, going through various designs before reaching maturity, and reliability in the AW three-speed hub of 1936. Here a central 'sun' gear was fixed to the axle, while 'planet' gears revolved around it, meshing with an inside-out gear ring lining the hub. The AW stands for 'all wide' giving a wide range of ratios: a middle gear which is direct drive; a low first gear where the wheel turns three times for every four revolutions of the sprocket; and a high third gear where the hub turns four times for every three revolutions of the sprocket. As a 1936 advert said, the Sturmey-Archer three speed was the 'neatest, lightest, cleanest' rear hub gear on offer.

Attached to the Raleigh 'All Steel' bicycle in various incarnations throughout the twentieth century, it became a world-beating combination. The bikes had 28-inch wheels, stainless steel spokes, long pedal cranks and long wheelbases, rod brakes and a fully enclosed chain. Extras included steering locks and hub dynamos. A black leather saddlebag was a finishing touch. They were, and are, virtually indestructible, and have been copied the world over, from the Indian Hero-Jet bicycle, to the Chinese Fei-Ge, or Flying Pigeon – of which over 500 million have been made. It shows its English ancestry by emblazoning 'All Steel' on its seat tube.

"THE BRITISH MASTERPIECE."

BIKES AND SOCIETY

GETTING AROUND
THE BICYCLE ACROSS THE GLOBE

Cycling's reputation is very often associated with leisure and childhood innocence. A sense of going on a bike ride as a slightly sweatier version of going for a weekend stroll. But cycling is all around us – on roads, in parks, in bike lanes. And our rather romanticised view of cycling ignores the profound impact it has made on society over the course of the twentieth century. In Beijing, China, nearly half of all journeys are made by bicycle. In Ferrara, Italy, cycling accounts for 30 per cent of journeys. In the U.K., York and Cambridge lead the way with just over a quarter of all trips made by bike. In The Netherlands – the home of the beloved Batavus sit-up-and-beg 'omafiets' or 'grandmother bike' – places like Groningen and Delft have more than half of all journeys made in the saddle.

A crossroads in
Copenhagen in 1930.
Today Copenhagen has a
reputation as perhaps the
most cycle-friendly city
in the world, with even
the postal service still
delivering mail by bike.

But while cycling has assumed global dimensions, it is also something that can
be seen as a reflection of national character. The Dutch grandmother bike is a
good example. In reality it was not Dutch at all, but a female version of a Dunlop
Safety Bicycle from the 1890s that the Dutch adopted and made their own. The
upright riding posture was immediately suited to the flat topography of Holland
– ideal for cruising alongside dykes. And in The Netherlands cycling maintained
a certain respectability, where elsewhere it was slowly overtaken by the car. For
the social historian Anne Ebert:

> *The tremendous success of the bicycle in the Netherlands can*
> *be at least partly explained by the particular way in which*
> *the bicycle was constructed and conceived as a promoter of*
> *Dutch national identity. To be Dutch meant to cycle, and this*
> *viewpoint remained prevalent until the Second World War,*
> *and – arguably to a lesser degree – remains so to this day.*

BICYCLE IN OTHER LANGUAGES

Welsh
BEIC

Danish
CYKEL

German
FAHRRAD

Dutch
FIETS

Italian
BICICLETTA

Turkish
BISIKLET

Yoruba
KEKE

The Netherlands remained, and still remains, very much a civic society, where who you are is bound up with a sense of a social role and social life. The Dutch, it can be argued, are much less individualistic than, say, Americans. Dutch bikes thus retain this social visibility: rather than the heads-down introspection of a racing bike, the upright posture allows one to easily nod, or doff one's cap, by way of greeting as you cycle past.

What is therefore interesting about the Dutch bike is how it has not changed over the decades. The Dutch were not particularly interested in innovation - the one-upmanship of extra gears or lighter frames. The Dutch bike therefore stands for a certain Protestant sense of earnest respectability, and a certain egalitarian vision - where all bikes are equal in the eyes of God. And this link to national character is shown by the popularity of cycling: there are more bikes than people in the Netherlands, and Amsterdam alone has 550,000 bikes versus 215,000 cars. To get rid of a bike - particularly your grandmother's or grandfather's bike - would be a little like ceasing to be Dutch.

Left In 1973, Dutch campaigners protested about the number of road deaths, leading to changes in road layouts in favour of cyclists.

Russian
VELOSIPED
(велосипед)

Japanese
JITENSHA
(自転車)

Chinese
ZI XING CHE
(自行车)

Indonesian
SEPEDA

China has often been referred to as the 'Kingdom of bicycles'. But bicycles took a while to catch on. Late nineteenth-century commentators were amazed that any self-respecting person would be willing to propel themselves around – why not take a sedan chair or a rickshaw? The bicycle was therefore only at first popular among certain sectors of society, like the 'sing-song' girls or concubines who used them to visit clients.

But the attractions of the bicycle soon prevailed, and Chinese bicycle manufacturing took off in the 1940s when the communists introduced affordable bicycles. By 1958, China was making over a million bicycles a year. Soon the bicycle was a symbol of prosperity and achievement. It became said that newlyweds needed 'three rounds and a sound': a watch, a bicycle, a sewing machine and a radio. In later decades Deng Xiaoping promised to put a Flying Pigeon in every home – referring to the ubiquitous single speed black roadster. Today, 400 factories produce 41 million bikes a year, in a country with a population of 1.3 billion, in total an estimated 370 million bicycles are in use.

But it is also this communist, centrally planned dimension to Chinese bicycle ownership that perhaps explains the resistance of current generations to their appeal. The Flying Pigeon, once the most populous vehicle on the planet, is now only produced in a quarter of its previous numbers. For young Chinese, bikes are a symbol of backwardness and poverty. Chinese bike ownership declined from 1995 to 2005 by 35 per cent, whereas car ownership doubled. Bikes are still seen on the streets of Chinese cities, but they haven't yet become the focus of a cycling revival, as in parts of Europe. Flying Pigeons are embroiled in a fatal daily battle with the car.

But in parts of the developing world the story is very different. In Africa, a bicycle still has the power to bring about a revolutionary change in people's daily lives. With a bike you can travel further to get water, to get medical supplies, to find work or attend school. But many imported bikes soon find themselves breaking down given the rigours of the conditions and the lack of skilled maintenance. The charity World Bicycle Relief has therefore been providing home-grown bicycles as an answer to the unreliablity of imported bikes. They call it the 'Buffalo' – symbolizing strength and power. It is designed to be able to carry 100 kg load. And it comes with a toolkit as a bike shop may be hundreds of miles away. While other parts of the world are only too keen to forget the bicycle, for many Africans it still represents a form of freedom and power.

Going to work on a bike: a crowded street in Beijing, with only a few hats, not helmets, in sight.

ZEN AND THE ART OF PUNCTURE REPAIR

It's a well-known fact of life that when you drop a piece of toast it will always land with the butter side down, and when you are unlucky enough to get a puncture it will never be near home or your destination. Equally, you are more likely to get a puncture when you're in a hurry than when you have all day to get to where you're going. These things are ruled by Sod's Law and there is nothing you can do about it. What you can affect is how you deal with it and this is where Zen comes in.

At the core of Zen is the practice of meditation, and remembering this when steam is coming out of your ears at yet another puncture will help you fix it quicker and, more importantly, fix it better. The moment you realise the air has been knocked out of your tyre - and your day - take a moment to put some air in your lungs. Breathe slowly and surely a few times before starting the repair. This breathing will slow your heart rate and, vitally, put some much-needed oxygen in your blood and thus calm your brain. Now you're relaxed you can get on with the repair.

THE PUNCTURE REPAIR KIT

Tyre levers

Patches

Sandpaper

Glue – if the patches don't have their own adhesive

Chalk – useful to mark where the hole is

Start off by removing the wheel from the bike. You may think it is not necessary but it makes the whole process much easier. If it's the rear wheel, make sure the bike is in the highest gear so that the chain is on the smallest sprocket. This will make removal and return simpler.

Before taking the tyre off have a close look to see if you can find out what has caused the puncture. If there is something stuck in it, carefully remove it. It's also worth noting where the puncture is, as it will be easier to find the hole in the inner tube.

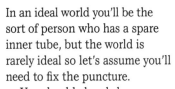

It's now time to unpack your trusty puncture repair kit and get one of those tyre levers out. After making sure the air is completely out of your tube, push the valve in to keep the tube out of harm's way and slip the flat end of the lever in under the rim inside the beading. Lever it outside the rim and hook the other end of the lever around a spoke. With part of the tyre now outside the rim, use another lever to work all around the tyre till it is totally free and then remove the inner tube.

In an ideal world you'll be the sort of person who has a spare inner tube, but the world is rarely ideal so let's assume you'll need to fix the puncture.

You should already have a good idea of where the hole is, but if you haven't noted it you'll find it easier to find if you put a bit of air back in. If the hole is really tiny you might even need to put the tube under water to see the bubbles of air coming out.

Once you've found the hole and marked it you should roughen the area around the hole with sandpaper. All good repair kits should have this, so check before you buy.

Apply the glue to an area bigger than your patch and allow the glue to dry somewhat. The patch won't stick otherwise. Once the patch is secured get that sandpaper out again and remove the excess glue. You don't want your inner tube sticking to your tyre!

Before putting the tube back on the wheel thoroughly check inside the tyre for anything sharp. Take care as it is easy, while running your fingers along the inside of the tyre, to cut yourself on some hidden sliver of glass. When you're happy there is nothing likely to re-puncture your tube, slip it inside the tyre. Start at the valve and its hole!

When the tube is fully in, pull the tyre back inside the rim making sure not to pinch the tube – you don't want to make another hole and have to start again. Start to inflate the tyre but don't go all the way without checking that the tyre is properly back inside the rim. Once you've checked this again put the wheel back on to the bike and then you can fully inflate the tube.

Remember to pack all your equipment away. It's easy to forget this and cycle off with a smile on your face only to get home and realise you've left your PRK on the pavement.

BICYCLES ON THE WARPATH

Despite being associated with tranquil excursions through peaceful countryside, bicycles have also played an important role in war throughout the twentieth century. Bicycles first saw action in the Boer War of 1899–1902, between the British and the combined forces of the South African Republic and the Orange Free State. A British General called Knox had made bicycles part of the compulsory basic training at Aldershot, and when war broke out a number of cycling corps were ready for action.

Unlike the Cavalry, however, there were certain things that could not be done on a bike. Soldiers mounted on horseback could shoot, with the horse able to withstand the recoil of a rifle, and were also able to swing a sword. But a soldier riding a bike was not really in a position to fight. Instead soldiers on bikes were deployed for a number of other purposes. They scouted to find roads suitable for transporting guns and equipment. They could be adapted to make stretcher bearers. Sometimes they were entrusted with special missions. In the run up to the war, a cyclist messenger during the Jameson Raid on the Transvaal Republic evaded detection by ingeniously concealing his despatches in his seatpost.

Fifteen years later, in the run up to the First World War, cyclists were actively recruited. One enlistment poster read:

> *Are You Fond of Cycling? If So, Why Not Cycle for the King? Recruits Wanted for the South Midland Divisional Cycling Company (must be 19 and willing to serve abroad). CYCLES PROVIDED. Uniform and Clothing issued on enlistment. Application in person or by letter to: Cyclists, The Barracks, Gloucester. BAD TEETH NO BAR.*

Presumably the reassurance about teeth was due to the fact that many cyclists - especially the riders of Penny Farthings - had lost a few teeth in the pursuit of their hobby.

Other European powers followed suit. In France, a number of military treatises were published discussing the tactical uses of bicycles. Bicycle adverts began to show soldier-cyclists on military manoeuvres. Germany responded by training army dogs to attack cyclists (do dogs need to be trained to do this?).

In Britain, a total of nine battalions of cyclists were commissioned around the time of the First World War, comprising around 14,000 men at the start of the war and over 100,000 by 1919. In the war, cycles served an expanded function. Many soldiers on bikes were used as scouts: they were faster than foot soldiers, and quieter than horses. And unlike a horse, a cycle laid on the ground was practically invisible. When it came to combat itself, cycle regiments mounted a form of guerilla warfare, attacking and retreating suddenly and stealthily, harassing and frustrating the enemy.

Key to all this, and of supreme importance to the serving infantryman, was the bike itself. How was it to be made suitable for military service? In the early years simple roadster bicycles were used, fitted with a storage box within the frame and a mount for carrying a Lee-Enfield bolt-action rifle. But in the Second World War, the British Army developed a new weapon – the BSA Paratrooper's Folding Airborne Bicycle. One of the problems of parachute warfare was the fact that drops might spread soldiers over a wide area – either because of wind conditions, or in order to reduce the risk of being spotted. Bicycles allowed them to regroup silently and swiftly. The bike design was lighter than a typical roadster, and folded via two wingnut hinges on the top and bottom tube. The handlebars folded and the pedals were simple spindles, allowing them too to be pushed out of the way. The bike weighed as little as 10 kg. Paratroopers strapped them to their chests as they jumped – to mount them on their backs would risk fouling the lines of the parachute. The bikes were made to be disposable, hidden away as the paratrooper approached the target. In total 60,000 of these folding troop transporters were made. Rather fittingly BSA stood for Birmingham Small

Left In a twist – a British Paratrooper with a BSA folding 'parabike'.

Far left Steel-helmeted German cycle corps celebrate Hitler's 50th birthday with a ride past on 20 April 1939.

Arms: the bike (and later motorbike) manufacturer who had started life as a rifle producer in 1861 in the aftermath of the Crimean War.

After the war the Folding Airborne Bicycle or 'parabike' lived on in various forms. BSA brought out a children's version with 20-inch wheels - non-folding, but with mudguards and a rack. And after surplus parabikes were sold to Denmark, the Danes copied the simple, effective design, making a bike suitable for civil defence duties during the Cold War, fitting a coaster drum brake, which gave this simple, effective bike even smoother lines.

For anyone wanting one of these mementos of the bicycle's role in wartime, they sometimes come up at auction - where they are worth many hundreds of pounds. Alternatively you can buy a modern replica made by Pashley, complete with very un-military 21-speed gears, mudguards, reflectors and bell.

'SMART LAD WANTED'
DELIVERY BOYS, BOBBIES AND POSTIES

In the olden days there would periodically appear a card in the windows of local butchers reading – 'Smart Lad Wanted for Delivery Round'. As well as playing an important role in the history of leisure, bikes have also played an important role in business over the twentieth century and keeping the wheels of capitalism moving. Hence the ever-presence of the delivery boy in early twentieth-century life, carrying a basketful of produce to the nation's homes – potatoes, carrots and tomatoes; newspapers, sausages and lamb chops.

The English novelist Arnold Bennett's 1911 novel *The Card* tells the story of a newspaper being bought out by an avaricious rival. In order to ensure the paper's success it imprisons its rival's delivery boys, thus showing the important role they played in the distribution of news. In the U.S. the iconic delivery boy, reaching into his shoulder bag and propelling the *Chicago Tribune* or the *Denver Post* onto the doormat, is an image as American as apple pie. While previously papers were sold only from newsstands, with the growth of the suburbs, the bicycling paper boy became a key part of American life – connecting this sprawling nation with itself. But the American paper boy is also an essential image of American-ness, of innocence, self-reliance and hard work: President Harry S. Truman, actors John Wayne and Bob Hope, as well as investment guru Warren Buffett, were all paper boys in their youth.

In England the figure of the French onion seller, or 'Onion Johnny' became a familiar figure over much of the twentieth century. Finding a more profitable market for their onions in England rather than at home, they crossed the channel in July, storing their onions in barns, before setting off for the highways and

byways of the home counties, their roadsters festooned with strings of pink Roscoff onions, berets on their heads. The peak of their trade was in the twenties and thirties, when over a thousand sellers imported 90,000 tons of onions. English housewives preferred the sweeter, stronger flavour of the French onions compared to the English varieties. For many people it was the only contact they would have had with someone from abroad, connecting them to the wider world.

Part of the reason for their journeying to England was linguistic. To these Breton speakers, English was as equally foreign to them as was Parisian French. A silent British comedy of the sixties called *San Ferry Ann*, telling of a bunch of Brits holidaying in France, climaxes in a scene of chaos caused by a French onion seller who spills his load on the road. It causes traffic mayhem, with cars and people slipping on the onions, and tears all round. The offending seller responds by chucking his bike in a river then jumping in after it.

But perhaps the occupations most associated with bicycling are that of the postman, and the English bobby, two perennial symbols of a world gone by.

Bicycles had been used by postal services the world over, but it was first in England that a bicycle was specifically designed for the job, the post office issuing a standardised design in 1929. Most were red but a head postmaster's bike was black. One interesting feature was the use of non-standard parts, to dissuade theft by passers-by, or by the postmen themselves. Many were made by the Cooperative Wholesale Society, and featured a GPO front lamp, saddle toolbag and beefy front rack capable of safely carrying 22kg. The rack was attached to the frame rather than the forks, so that it would not affect handling on tricky descents. An allowance of 1 shilling a month was paid to posties for maintenance and repairs. An issue of the magazine *Cycling* from 1941 pays tribute to this trusty machine:

Telegrams may encircle the globe within a few seconds; photographs may be despatched from New York and received in London within the shortest measure of time; motor vehicles and special express trains may transport thousands of letters to all parts of the country. But there is still a place in the scheme of things for the bicycle.

And not far behind the postman was the English bobby. At first English police officers used their own cycles, but soon they became as essential a part of police equipment as truncheons and handcuffs. In 1896, the East Riding of Yorkshire Constabulary purchased 12 bicycles, fitted with Dunlop tyres, bags, bells and lamps for the sum of £12 16s. Other local forces followed suit, and soon the 'bobby' on a bike was a familiar sight. In later years the Raleigh DL-1 Roadster was a popular choice, with 28-inch wheels, rod brakes, rear dynamo and battery pack for powering the lights at standstill. And only one large frame size was needed: historically policemen were required to be at least 5ft 10, and in the City of London at least six foot tall.

Above Breton onion sellers in South Wales in 1938.

Right Bicycling Bobby: a policemen sets off on his beat in the 1940s.

'ELASTIC AND ACTIVE'
ANNIE LONDONDERRY AND RATIONAL CLOTHING

It is fair to say that one of the most important pieces of equipment for a keen cyclist is what they wear. Cyclists need to stay warm, but also reduce drag. They need to combine practicality and visibility. But they also need to remain flexible: the sort of boots and clothing that might keep one dry on a hill walk would be totally unsuitable for swinging one's leg over a bike.

But in the early days of cycling, this challenge was compounded by an additional factor. Bikes were emancipatory, freeing men from the drudgery of city life, but they also gave freedom to women. Bikes allowed them to escape from the home – their supposed preoccupation – and allowed them to travel for next to nothing. A woman on a bicycle did not need to find the money for a cab, and bikes were less expensive to maintain than a horse. Bikes thus began to give women physical and financial independence. In 1896, The American suffragette Susan B. Anthony claimed that the bicycle 'has done more to emancipate women than anything else in the world'.

However, riding a bike also presented a challenge to traditional notions of femininity. Women were expected to ride side-saddle on horses in the nineteenth century. Sitting astride something was seen as an implicitly sexual act, and one that all respectable ladies should avoid. One French medical 'expert' even commented that cycling would ruin the 'feminine organs of matrimonial necessity'. Some side-saddle bikes were invented, but they were, as you would expect, barely functional.

'I think you need to change gear'. The impracticality of ladies' clothing is shown as one woman helps another to regain her balance in 1885.

A concession to decorum was made by the Stanley firm in 1889, when it introduced the Stanley 'Psycho Ladies' Bicycle' – basically a Safety Bicycle with a step-through frame, a design that lives on to the present day. A woman was thus relieved of the supposed indignity of having to swing her leg. But the basic problem of cycling in women's traditional skirts and dresses remained. Cycling in such clothing was also downright dangerous. A Cheltenham resident wrote to the *Daily Mail* in April 1897 to tell of how:

> [...] *two young ladies were riding side by side, It was very windy, and the skirt of one blew into the wheel of the other, where it got caught. They both turned somersaults. When they were picked up, their skirts were very nearly taken off them – well, I found it necessary to look the other way.*

But another letter to the *Daily Press* in September 1896 struck a far more serious tone. It told of the death of a Miss Carr in Cumbria. Her friend reported that while out cycling 'Miss Carr began a descent with her feet in the rests but finding the hill become much steeper she strove to regain her pedals and failed'. The letter-writer commented: 'I think she failed because she could not

Cycles et Automobiles Legia

P. Deprez Scassart
Herstal (Liège)
Belgium Cycles

AFF. D'ART O. DE RYCKER & MENDEL BRUXELLES

see the pedals, as the flapping skirt hid them from her view, and she had to fumble for them. Could she have taken but a momentary glance at their position, she would have had a good chance to save her life. The poor girl lingered a week.'

Hence the creation of the Rational Clothing Movement, founded in 1881 to further the cause of female dress reform and in which cycling was a key issue. One American proponent, Frances E. Willard, commented on the power of the bicycle to erode prejudices about what women are allowed to wear on a bike, and consequently wear at home:

If women ride they must, when riding, dress more rationally than they have been wont to do. If they do this many prejudices as to what they may be allowed to wear will melt away. Reason will gain upon precedent, and ere long the comfortable, sensible, and artistic wardrobe of the rider will make the conventional style of woman's dress absurd to the eye and unendurable to the understanding.

While some men found women in 'bifurcated' clothing an abomination, others approved. Hoopdriver, the hero of H.G. Wells's *Wheels of Chance*, comments on the young woman in Rational dress that he meets out cycling: 'she didn't look a bit unwomanly... How fine she had looked, flushed with the exertion of riding, breathing a little fast, but elastic and active! Talk about your ladylike, homekeeping girls with complexions like cold veal!'

The figurehead of the Rational Clothing and of women's cycling more generally was Annie 'Londonderry' Kopchovsky, who in 1896 became the first woman to cycle around the world. Significantly, she chose to do this to settle a bet, not only to circle the globe in fifteen months, but to earn $5000 dollars on the way – a test of a woman's physical power, but also her financial self-reliance. She gained her nickname from the Londonderry Lithia Water Company that paid her $100 to carry its advertising on her bike. She set off from Boston in 1894, according to one observer sailing 'like a kite down Beacon Street'. She rode a 19kg Columbia bicycle and wore men's clothing for most of the way. Her success was a huge victory for bicycling, but also for women more generally. In an interview with the *Omaha World Herald* she said that 'in the near future all women, whether of high or low degree, will bestride the wheel.'

Above Annie Londonderry posing, this time skirted, in a photographic studio *c.*1900. But note the step-through frame.

Left A woman wearing 'bifurcated' clothing – bloomers – in an advert for Legia cars and bicycles of 1898.

A CENTURY OF

'If you build it, they will come' is a well-known misquote from a film about baseball, and it serves us quite well when we look at how bicycle manufacture and the industrial revolution went very much hand in hand.

Above Like a wheel within a wheel, a Raleigh factory worker shows off his wares.

Right Thousands of Raleigh bicycles lined up and ready to go in the 1980s.

The development of the Safety Bicycle was a vital step away from transport involving horses and carriages and allowed people, initially mainly working men, to travel reasonable distances with a bit of speed. This allowed them to work in major towns and cities and helped the development of the industrial processes that led to the mass manufacture of the parts needed to make the bike available to all.

The first actual factory for the production of bicycles was run by the Michaux family in Paris, France. The company was already established as a manufacturer of coaches when they started producing bicycles in the 1860s. It was a Michaux bicycle that was brought back to Coventry by a travelling salesman that led to the establishment of the first bicycle factory in the U.K.

Rowley Turner was the sales agent for the Coventry Sewing Machine Company in Paris, and his uncle, Josiah Turner, was a company director. When nephew encouraged uncle to diversify into bikes, by placing the first order himself (which he planned to sell to the French market), bicycle manufacturing in the U.K. was born. In fact, so successful did this side of the business become that by the late 1860s the company's name had changed to Coventry Machinists Company and by the mid 1880s it had stopped sewing machine manufacture altogether.

This one company was the birthplace of several factories with employees from here moving on to set up Bayliss, Thomas & Co., Centaur Cycle Co., Smith, Starley & Co. and Hillman, Herbert and Cooper, among others. The greenhouse effect of this meant that Coventry quickly established itself as the centre of world bicycle manufacturing. It was among these verdant chimneys that the greatest breakthrough saw the light of day, namely the Rover Safety Bicycle (see page 20).

MANUFACTURING

The introduction and success of the safety bike was the spark that ignited the flames for the golden age of cycling. One of the few companies that sprang up during this period and is still running is the Raleigh Bicycle Company. Founded in Nottingham, it was named after the street in which the first factory was opened. Almost simultaneously across the Atlantic in the United States an important organisation was formed which had the aim of promoting the interests of cyclists. The League of American Wheelmen was formed in 1880 with the specific point of campaigning for paved roads. Within 20 years they had over 100,000 members. The first large scale manufacturer in the States was Albert Pope's company in Boston, but it was Adolph Schoeninger's Western Wheel Works, formerly a toy company, which really started mass-production with its innovation of stamping to replace the slower and more expensive process of machining the main parts. In 1891 they made more than 25,000 bikes and

RALEIGH B.S.A. 'TOUR-DE-FRANCE'
10-speed gears
[H]

£96·95
£2·56
for 38 wks

10-SPEED DERAILLEUR GEARS.
MAES-PATTERN HANDLEBARS.
WEINMANN CENTRE-PULL BRAKES
WITH HOODED LEVERS.
LARGE-FLANGE HUBS.
TOE CLIPS WITH STRAPS
AND WATER BOTTLE.

22½-in FRAME
SUITABLE FOR
INSIDE LEG
31½ to 33½ ins

Left Riding the 'same' bicycle as the pros was possible on the drip!

Right As manufacturing declined in the West the world's demand for bikes was met in the East. This is the production line of Diamond Back mountain bikes at the China Bicycle Company in Shenzhen Economic Zone in 1994.

this had increased to 55,000 just four years later. Their biggest seller was the Crescent which was specifically marketed to women riders, with the new-shaped frame missing the top tube, thus making it easier to be ridden in the voluminous dresses of the day.

It is a sad thing that so many inventions and innovations come as a result of war, but we cannot ignore the impact of the Great War. One company in particular in the U.K. that made great strides in the war years was the Birmingham Small Arms Company. Up until 1908 BSA, as they were commonly referred to, had only produced bicycle parts, but from this year they went into the production of finished bicycles. They quickly became a big supplier of cycles to the police and the army and during the war they introduced a bike that could be folded and carried on a soldier's back (see page 97). In fact most armies had at least one bicycle infantry. Obviously, given their name, they also supplied arms to the army including probably its most famous weapon, the Lewis Gun.

With the economic strictures imposed by the conflict, the war also led to a further boost in cycling at home because it was still such a cheap form of transport. This growth continued when peace returned and with a new-found workforce, the women who had been forced into factories, output was continually increasing. Raleigh, for instance, was producing half a million cycles a year by the end of the 1930s. This rise was halted suddenly with the outbreak of the Second World War, with the factories that had been producing cycles being forced into making items for the war effort. Raleigh's factory output of bikes went down to just 5 per cent of the total production.

Bicycles were still present in the conflict but were superseded by their motorised cousins, and this was a harbinger of the fate of pedal power after the war. Not necessarily a harbinger of doom, but a warning that the need for bikes would change. Up until the Second World War the bicycle had been used mainly as a necessity for getting to work, for delivering goods and so on, but this changed from the 1950s. With the growth of motorbikes and cars and a gradual increase in wealth, the need to have the cheapest form of transport reduced. This could have been the death knell for the bicycle but it wasn't – it just created a shift in usage from business to leisure.

The shift into leisure and sports use meant that innovation and diversification became a vital part of keeping the industry afloat. When bikes had just been used to get to and from work, they needed to be built and designed in a very particular, similar way. With new uses varying from off-roading to racing via trick-cycling the shape and look of the bike became much more varied. This led to a split on the manufacturing side between at one end the mass-market off-the-shelf bikes made at huge factories, to the other end with artisan bike makers building individual machines to order. And so while all bikes can still be traced back to the Rover Safety, the way they are made now is as assorted as the many number of uses that can be dreamed up.

BICYCLES AND THE ART OF ADVERTISING

The art of advertising grew up alongside the bicycle. The first bikes were expensive items. In 1883, a Penny Farthing cost £12 10s, five months' work for an agricultural labourer. Over time the price of bikes came down, as more manufacturers entered the market and production became increasingly mechanised. But a bike remained an expensive investment – in Vittorio de Sica's *Bicycle Thieves* (1948), a wife and husband pawn their wedding presents in order that he might buy a bike. The tempting medium of advertising was therefore a key ingredient in the success of the bicycle in the early days.

An old American advert for a 'Scorcher Safety Bicycle – Best and Most Popular' from 1892, gives a flavour of the first bicycle ads. The unfamiliarity of the form of the bicycle is shown in the rather sketchy drawing: the frame wheels and handlebars seem out of proportion; the chainwheel and chain are barely recognizable. The bicycle appears as a new, almost alien thing. But the name also shows the manufacturer's awareness of this growing young market. 'Scorcher' was the slang name for the reckless young men who rode these machines at breakneck speed, without consideration for other vehicles or pedestrians. Yet the manufacturers seem to be seizing on this notoriety, boasting proudly: 'Agents wanted everywhere'.

Other adverts concentrated on the sporting pedigree of their machines. A poster for Alcyon

SCORCHER SAFETY BICYCLES
BEST AND MOST POPULAR.

Genuine Imported Weldless Steel used throughout its construction.
AGENTS WANTED EVERYWHERE.
BRETZ & CURTIS MF'G CO.,
Philadelphia, Pa., U. S. A.
SEND FOR CATALOGUE,   Mention this paper.

Above An early advert for Scorcher Safety Bicycles, 1892 – 'Scorcher' refers to young men who rode at breakneck speeds.

A lithographic poster for Alcyon bicycles, using Tour de France champion François Faber to promote the sporting quality of their bikes.

This beautiful lithograph captures the place of the bicycle in the changing times at the turn of the century, with a modern style that embodies clever advertising and visual appeal.

Left This beautiful lithograph captures the place of the bicycle in the changing times at the turn of the century, with a modern style that embodies clever advertising and visual appeal.

Cycles of Neuilly-sur-Seine shows the champion cyclist François Faber bearing down on the viewer. Faber, born in Luxembourg, was the first foreigner to win the Tour de France, in 1909, and his record of winning five consecutive stages still stands. The poster represents all the confidence and optimism of cycling in the pre-war days (Faber was to die during the Battle of Artois near Arras, in 1915). But what is also interesting is the skill of the artist, as shown in the perfect foreshortening of Faber's arms and legs, but also his artistic licence – the white handlebars form the 'Y' in the name 'Alcyon', picked out in serpentine art nouveau lettering. Alcyon went on to dominate the Tour de France in the twenties and thirties, along with riders such as Nicolas Frant and Maurice De Waele.

As well as being associated with sporting masculinity, bikes were also advertised for, and by, women, often with humour at men's expense. One advert for 'Fucosine' anti-puncture fluid, boasts 'Enough of Flat Tyres' and shows a clear sense of female one-upmanship, as a young woman whizzes past a punctured male cyclist. She rides skilfully one-handed, holding flowers in one hand and a bottle of 'Fucosine' in the other. The male rider kneels on the verge, feeling deflated at not only his breakdown, and his injured pride, but also at the loss of that traditional male prerogative – helping stranded damsels to fix their bikes.

Occasionally, bicycle adverts approach the status of fine art. A mesmerizing lithograph by Eugène Grasset for Georges Richard bikes provides a good example. Grasset, of Swiss-French descent, was one of the most influential art nouveau artists of the Belle Epoque era. Georges Richard was a respected cycle maker who offered lifetime guarantees on his bikes. But in the poster, Grasset has had the bravery to demote the bike itself to the bottom right-hand side of the frame. Instead, a beautiful flame-haired woman occupies the main body, contrasting with bands of browns and greens in the background, suggesting landscape but also movement. But the woman's and the poster's focus is on a four-leafed clover – Georges Richard's logo – that she holds in her hand. Grasset has taken the logo, and made it real, but also made it unreal again, placing its blue leaves within a white circle, turning it into a bicycle wheel, but also a symbol of the naturalness and good fortune of bicycling itself.

BLAZING SADDLES

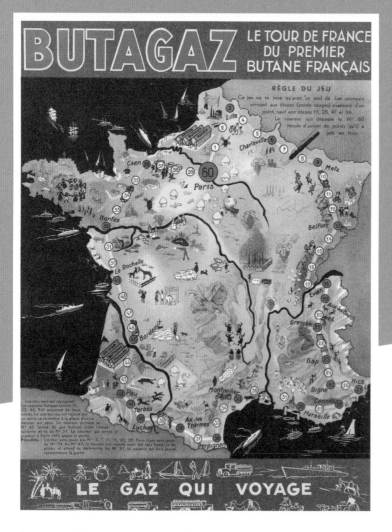

LE TOUR DE FRANCE

In football there is the World Cup, for dogs there's Crufts and for cycling and cyclists the pinnacle of achievement is Le Tour de France. Like the football and canine championships you don't need to name the sport or go into any detail; just saying 'Le Tour' is enough for people all over the world to know what you mean. It is the ultimate test of cycling stamina, speed, skill and, above all else, endurance.

Le Tour was conceived in 1902 by Géo Lefèvre, the cycling correspondent at the failing daily sports paper *L'Auto*, as a way to gain readers over its chief rival *Le Vélo*. This, rather bizarrely, was a sports newspaper rivalry that came about thanks to the non-cycling controversy of the Dreyfus Affair, but that's another story. While it was Lefèvre's idea, it was the paper's editor Henri Desgrange who actually put the race on the road – and it was he who ran it like his personal property until illness forced him to stop in 1936. Over the course of those years he took Lefèvre's concept and moulded it into one of the world's biggest and widely followed sporting events.

The first race was held in 1903 at the end of May and beginning of June over six stages, and was a total of 1,509 miles (2,428 km) long. There were 84 competitors although only 60 competed over the whole course, the rest limiting themselves to one or more stages. That first Tour was won by Frenchman Maurice Garin, who also won three of the six stages. He crossed the line first in the second Tour too, although was later stripped of that title amidst claims of cheating (including at one point catching a train).

It wasn't only Garin who was disqualified from the second Tour. During the race itself nine riders were eliminated for a variety of reasons and once the dust had settled the French cycling union investigated allegations from a number of cyclists against their fellow competitors. The result was that every stage winner, who actually made up three of the first four overall was disqualified (Garin, Hippolyte Aucouturier and Lucien Pothier) plus the fourth in the top four, César Garin. This left 19-year-old Henri Cornet as the winner.

The level of cheating, gamesmanship and general lack of sporting behaviour threatened to make the second Tour the last. The event was temporarily put on hold and the 1905 (third) tour was only held after new rules were put in place to try to make the event easier to referee. The stage lengths were reduced so that no night racing was needed, the number of stages was increased to eleven and the winner was decided on a points system rather than time.

This third tour was also important in the race's development because it was the first to see the cyclists head up into the mountains. It is the mountain stages that really set the Tour apart from other races, and they have become as important to its success as the bunched sprint finishes.

In the formative years Desgrange tinkered with how the winner was decided. Initially it was decided on the total time taken, but from 1906 to 1912 a points system for stage placings was used. Desgrange was not really happy with either of these, believing that both had inequities. The former could see someone knocked out of contention with just one terrible day while the latter made only the end of each stage important, so that riders could pootle along, preserving energy for the last few kilometres when the actual race would start. This was not the severe test of human endurance that the race was designed for.

For many years Desgrange attempted to battle against the influence of the teams, believing that the race should be about individuals. While riders were mainly entered and supported by the factories, Desgrange did not believe that they should be allowed to interfere with the race itself. This extended to riders having to mend their bikes themselves and, until 1923, keeping the same machine for the whole race. Right up until a prostate operation in 1936 stopped his involvement with the race, Desgrange battled against the influence of the factories and their teams. It would be interesting to hear his opinion on the race as it is now, being so dominated by teams - and more specifically team tactics - promoting just one rider among them to become the eventual winner. The fact of the matter is that in spite of his hatred of them, it is the bicycle manufacturers that have kept the Tour going.

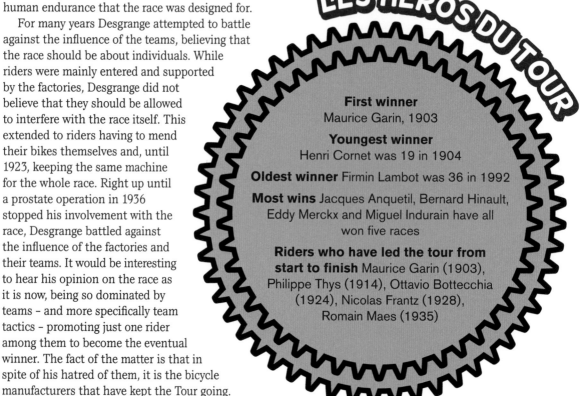

LES HÉROS DU TOUR

First winner
Maurice Garin, 1903

Youngest winner
Henri Cornet was 19 in 1904

Oldest winner Firmin Lambot was 36 in 1992

Most wins Jacques Anquetil, Bernard Hinault, Eddy Merckx and Miguel Indurain have all won five races

Riders who have led the tour from start to finish Maurice Garin (1903), Philippe Thys (1914), Ottavio Bottecchia (1924), Nicolas Frantz (1928), Romain Maes (1935)

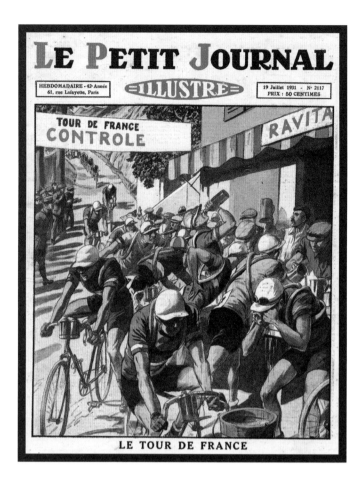

LE TOUR DE FRANCE

It is difficult, maybe impossible, to think about Le Tour without some mention of Lance Armstrong. From 1999 to 2005 he dominated the race like no other rider. Four riders (Jacques Anquetil, Eddy Merckz, Bernard Hinault and Miguel Indurain) have won the tour five times, but no one has won six and only Armstrong has won seven, plus his wins were in consecutive years. This was a superhuman effort and gained him fans and adoration around the globe. It is interesting to look at the official statistics now that Lance Armstrong has been wiped off the face of the cycling world. While the Second World War meant that there were no winners recorded for the seven years from 1940 to 1946, Armstrong's drug-fuelled efforts have left the same sized gap in the record books. The legacy of the Armstrong years is not just seven blanks where the winners' names should be. Each year now the victor and his efforts are scrutinised for any sign that he may be in breach of the doping rules.

It is amazing that such a massive sporting event could have been brought almost to its knees by one man, but that is what has happened. It is the job of the UCI and all the cyclists and their teams to make sure that the sport is clean - and shown to be so. Millions follow the progress of the race either in person, on television, online and via social networks and they all want to be assured that the race they love is the toughest examination of human endurance and effort, and that the winner of it stands on the podium thanks to his own efforts, unaided by the contents of a needle.

Like the other Grand Tours, the original is dominated by the host nation, with 36 wins having come from home soil. Belgium, Spain and Italy account for 40 between them with the rest being shared among nine countries. Amazingly it took Great Britain until 2012 to win it for the first time, thanks to Sir Bradley Wiggins – just plain old Bradley at the time. Chris Froome's two wins were quickly added in 2013 and 2015.

As Le Tour heads into its second century it goes from strength to strength, helped by the growing popularity of cycling both as a sport and leisure activity. You may not want to do it yourself, but there are not many sports where any enthusiast can follow the route taken by their heroes and put themselves through the same trials, but this, the first of the great road races, allows just that possibility.

GIRO D'ITALIA

Six years after a circulation war in France saw the creation of that country's Tour, it was again battling newspapers that led to the arrival of the second of what we now call the Grand Tours. *La Gazzetta dello Sport*, as its name suggests, is a newspaper that only covers sport, but it still competed with traditional papers which carried sport as well as news. When it was rumoured that one of its rivals, *Corriere della Sera*, was planning a cycle race, *La Gazzetta* jumped in first.

THE JERSEY NO ONE WANTED

For a short time (1946–1951) a black jersey – *La Maglia Nera* – was worn by the rider at the bottom of the General Classification.

La Gazzetta had already had great success with two smaller races over the previous few years; Giro di Lombardia and Milano–San Remo, and so on 7 August 1908 the paper announced the first Giro D'Italia would be held the following year. Starting on 13 May 1909 there were 127 riders who would compete over 8 stages. The overall winner of the first tour was decided by a points system with the winner of each stage receiving 1 point, second place 2 points and so on. Thus the overall winner was the rider with the fewest points, having completed every stage. Only 49 riders lasted the full 1,521 miles (2,448 km).

The first stage in the inaugural Giro was from Milan to Bologna and was the longest stage that year, covering a massive 246 miles (397 km). Luigi Ganna finished fourth in that first stage and was second in the second stage, putting him at the top of the general classification. Other than after the mountainous third stage he stayed at the head of the General Classification all the way to the finish back in Milan on 30 May, beating second-placed Carlo Galetti by just two points. Unlike the present day where riders barely have a rest day, the first Giro was spread over two and a half weeks with racing only taking place on Thursdays, Sundays and Tuesdays.

Galetti's near miss in the first Giro spurred him on and he won the next two races beating 100 other riders in 1910 and 85 a year later - when the total distance had increased to 2,191 miles (3,526 km) over 12 stages. Galetti was denied a possible hat-trick of victories when the organisers decided that the 1912 race would be competed solely by teams and not individuals. It seems a perverse decision even now and was hotly disputed at the time. The rationale was that although an individual winner could be determined it was, in effect, impossible

BINDA'S 1927 MONOPOLY

In 1927 Alfredo Binda won 12 out of the 15 stages! This is still a record. He also jointly holds the record of 5 Giro victories with Fausto Coppi and Eddy Merckx.

THE ONE AND ONLY

Alfonsina Strada is the only woman to ever compete in the Giro. In 1924 she entered as Alfonsin Strada when a dispute with the teams led to the Giro allowing individuals to apply for a place. By the time it was discovered she was not a he, it was too late and she was allowed to ride.

for someone to win the race without the help of his team. Therefore it seemed obvious to have it as a team competition rather than an individual one.

The teams consisted of four riders, of which three had to finish each stage to remain in the competition. The winning team was still to be decided on a points system with four going to the team who provided the stage winner, any team with two riders in the top four would receive a further two points and every team received a point for having three finishers on any stage. As well as the controversy of this change the race was clouded by the fourth stage being annulled when the riders took the wrong route and ended up nowhere near the actual stage climax at a stadium in Rome!

This one-off experiment ended with Galetti and Ganna's Atala team taking the Giro, with the help of their two teammates Giovanni Micheletto and Eberardo Pavesi. The following year's tour reverted to the previous format, to everyone's delight, but this only lasted a year before the final and fundamental change to the winner being decided on overall time.

The first 'time' winner was Alfonso Calzolari who beat his nearest competitor by 1 hour, 57 minutes and 26 seconds. This is still a record-winning margin by nearly a full hour! This is partly explained by the fact that only 8 riders finished the 8 stages, which had a punishing average length of nearly 250 miles (400 km). This is over twice the average stage distance of the current tour. The conditions throughout the race were awful, mainly due to heavy rainfall. Calzolari was already over an hour ahead after just a quarter of the race and the riders were dropping like flies.

LA DOMENICA DEL CORRIERE

Supplemento settimanale illustrato del nuovo CORRIERE DELLA SERA *- Spedizione in abbonamento postale · Gruppo 2°*

Anno 61 — N. 22   31 Maggio 1959   L. 40.—

Far left In 2012, Ryder Hesjedal became the first Canadian to wear the Giro's Pink Jersey.

Left The riders on the streets of Milan at the start of the first Giro, as illustrated by Achille Beltrame.

STANDING ROOM ONLY

The 1928 tour had the most starters in the race's history with 298 riders rolling out of Milan. The smallest number to compete was 56 in 1912.

A WHISKER

The 1948 race was almost too close to call, with Fiorenzi Magni beating Ezio Cecchi by just 11 seconds over a tour which lasted 124 hours, 51 minutes and 52 seconds.

Calzolari's win in 1914 meant that he held the title until 1919 because the race was not held again until after the Great War. On resumption, Italy's dominance was maintained and would continue until 1950 when the victor's spoils finally left the Tour's home and went to Switzerland with Hugo Koblet. Since the Italian monopoly was broken ten further countries have provided the winner, but Italy still dominates with 68 victories compared to the next best of 7 for Belgium.

The leader and eventual winner of the Giro gets the honour of wearing the Pink Jersey, *La Maglia Rosa*. The colour was introduced in 1931 and was chosen in honour of the newspaper that started the race – *La Gazzetta* is printed on pink paper.

Left Spain's isolation while under Franco's rule meant that the Vuelta was often not raced during his tenure.

Below Racers hurtling past the Royal Palace in Madrid.

VUELTA A ESPAÑA

They say good things come in threes – and after a wait of nearly thirty years two tours became three in 1935 when Spain provided its very own Grand Tour to add to those of France and Italy. As with its older siblings, the Spanish race came into being initially as a means to boost the circulation of a newspaper. Sadly, unlike the periodicals that gave birth to the two other Grand Tours, 'Informaciones' is no longer in circulation having closed for business in 1983. At least it is still remembered thanks to the race it fostered – which is still going strong.

The early years of the Vuelta a España were a little faltering, coming as they did at a time of global, and national, political upheaval. The first two races were won by the Belgian rider Gustaaf Deloor, ahead of relatively small fields. The entry numbers suffered due to the proximity to the already well-established Giro d'Italia. In 1935 the Vuelta finished on 15 May with the Giro starting on the 18th, making entry into both pretty much impossible, and in 1936 the races actually overlapped. From the start the Vuelta was a timed race, its organisers having learned the lessons from the early experiments of the other tours. Deloor won the first race, over 2,147 miles (3,455 km), by just over 12 minutes, and the second by just under 12 minutes.

When Deloor crossed the finishing line on 31 May 1936, the start of the Spanish Civil War was just six weeks away. The conflict that ravaged the country lasted nearly three years and it wasn't for another two years that the Vuelta started up again. It was surprising that the 1941 version happened at all given that it came in the middle of the Second World War. Because of this it was hardly a shock that there were only 32 starters for this isolated event, but it did bring the first home victory, for Julián Berrendero Martín. He repeated the feat the next year against

a slightly larger field of 40. The raging Second World War finally put a stop to the tour but only for one year. Amazingly just two days after VE Day the Vuelta started in Madrid and produced another Spanish winner, Delio Rodríguez Barros.

The stop-start nature of the Vuelta's early years did not end with the coming of world peace. Having been ruled by Francisco Franco since 1936, a power consolidated with victory in the Civil War, the end of the Second World War saw Spain feeling the effects of its economic and political isolation. This resulted once more in the race suffering a hiatus that only came to end when, in 1955, international relations improved and Spain was given entry in to the United Nations.

The 1955 revival was to all intents and purposes a rebirth for the race and again it was thanks to the media, on this occasion the Basque newspaper *El Correo Español*. This new version of the race saw a record field of 106 starters, twice as many as any previous race. It was also the shortest up to that point with a distance of *only* 1,725 miles (2,776 km) over 15 stages.

So finally, after 20 years of faltering first steps, the Vuelta was up and running and has been an integral part of the annual cycling calendar ever since. As with the other two Tours it has been dominated by the home nation, but not quite to the same extent. Of the 69 races, 32 have thrown up Spanish wins, with France, next best, providing 9 wins. Roberto Heras of Spain has won the race four times

Only six riders have
achieved the career triple crown.
The first rider to win all three Grand
Tours at least once was the Frenchman
Jacques Anquetil, who completed the feat in
1963 with his Vuelta victory. This elite group is
made up of Felice Gimondi (Italy), Eddy Merckx
(Belgium), Bernard Hinault (France), Alberto
Contador (Spain) and Vincenzo Nibali (Italy).
Of these, only Hinault and Contador have won
each race more than once. Hinault did in fact
win the three tours consecutively but not in the
same year, while Merckx won four in a row,
but again not in the one year.

CROWNING GLORY

(in 2000, 2003, 2004 and 2005). His last
win was clouded with drugs controversy
such that he had the title stripped and it was
handed to the Russian runner-up Denis Menchov.
After legal appeals regarding the validity of the testing,
a Spanish court ruled in 2011 that Heras was the rightful winner
but the UCI has yet to change its records. Two riders have won it three times,
Tony Rominger of Switzerland and Alberto Contador of Spain.

The longest Vuelta was one of the early ones, the 1941 version, which covered
2,738 miles (4,406 km) over 21 stages. The greatest margin of victory came four
years later when Delio Rodríguez Barros came home half an hour ahead of the
field. The smallest margin of victory was a meagre 6 seconds in 1984 for Eric
Caritoux. In 1977, Freddy Maertens won 13 of the 19 stages to secure the red
jersey. The next best for any winner is just 6.

The Vuelta stubbornly stuck to an end of April/start of May running period
that kept it in too close a proximity to the Giro until 1995, when it moved to a
September start. Even with this change, very few riders complete all three Tours.
Up to the 1995 change of date there were only 28 completed rides in all three
tours in the same year. The change has not actually made much difference with
only a further 13 riders doing the hat-trick. No rider has ever won all three Tours
in the same year. In fact, of the 41 occasions on which a rider has completed all
three in the same year there has only been a single tour victory. In 1957, Gastone
Nencini won the Giro and finished 6th and 9th in the Tour and the Vuelta
respectively. The only other rider to finish in the top ten in all 3 in the same year
was Raphael Geminiani in 1955. It is so difficult that generally riders will focus
on two or, more likely, one of the three Tours in any one year and use one of the
others as preparation.

THE GREATEST RACERS
FROM INDURAIN TO MERCKX

Who is the greatest rider in the history of cycling? It is a question that all keen cyclists ask, but about which all disagree. In terms of the history of cycling, it may be the estimable Thomas Stevens, who rode round the world on a Penny Farthing. In terms of all round ability, it may be Marianne Vos, the female Dutch cyclist who holds titles in cyclo-cross, road racing, mountain biking and track. But whenever cyclists gather together to discuss the greatest there has ever been, three names invariably come up: Indurain, Coppi and Merckx.

Miguel Indurain was the first cyclist to win five straight Tour de France victories, which he won between 1991 and 1995 (Lance Armstrong won seven from 1999 to 2005, but was stripped of the titles in 2012 for doping). Indurain was born near Pamplona, in Spain, on 16 July 1964, a farmer's son. He became Spanish National Champion in 1983 and turned professional two years later. He came to the world's attention on the Tour of 1991 (he had finished tenth the year before). Up until that point the modest, quietly spoken Indurain had been considered a good team rider. But during 1991 he stepped up the pace. Known for his mountain riding previously, Indurain won the 73 km time trial from Argentan to Alencon in the first week. He went on to win overall, following this with an amazing four wins in the following years.

What is also remarkable about Indurain is his size and weight for a professional cyclist: 6ft 2 (1.88 m) weighing 12½ stone (80 kg). Although carrying more weight than other riders, it also gave 'Big Mig', as he came to be known, a great deal of power. Cycling fitness basically comes down to how much oxygen can be delivered to the leg muscles. Indurain was helped by superior natural physical capacities. The average male's resting heart rate is 72 beats per minute with a lung capacity of 4.8 litres. Indurain, by contrast, possessed a resting heart rate of 28 beats per minute and a lung capacity of 7.8 litres. In addition, Indurain was blessed with a very high Vo2 max rating – the highest volume of oxygen that can be consumed during exercise. Indurain's rating was 88 ml/kg/min – double that of most men and women, anything above 70 being considered 'elite'. It is reported that during one test at Navarre University, Indurain broke the 'wattbike' used to test physical capacity. 'Big Mig', this horse of a man on a bike, undoubtedly possessed immense physical strength. But he also displayed a modesty that many found remarkable for a man of his fame and achievement. One teammate said that when he sat down next to you for a meal, 'you don't even hear him move his chair'.

Left Miguel Indurain in the mountains on the Tour de France in 1993.

Below Indurain takes a corner at speed on the Tour of 1990.

Angelo Fausto Coppi dominated road racing during the middle years of the twentieth century. He was a great all-rounder – sprinter, time trialler, and mountain climber. He won the Giro d'Italia five times between 1940 and 1953, the Tour de France twice (in '49 and '52), as well as the World Championship in '53.

Coppi was born in Piedmont, Italy, in September 1919. He was not particularly athletic as a child, having suffered malnutrition, but after school found a job as a butcher's errand boy. He was cycling daily, and climbing the stairs to customers' apartments strengthened his legs. Soon his interest in cycling bloomed, and an uncle gave him 600 lire to buy a made-to-measure racing bike. He won his first race at the age of 15, winning 20 lire and a salami sandwich. Four years later, with a racing licence, he won an alarm clock.

His first major achievement was winning the Giro D'Italia at the age of 20 in 1940, but the outbreak of war interrupted his career. He served in North Africa, eventually becoming a prisoner of the British, during which time he became the camp barber. After the war, Coppi began to dominate cycling, with his gangly legs earning him the nickname *Il Airone* or The Heron. It is said that between the years '46–'54 when Coppi broke from the pack he was never once caught. The French racer Raphaël Géminiani said of him:

> When Fausto won and you wanted to check the time gap to the man in second place, you didn't need a Swiss stopwatch. The bell of the church clock tower would do the job just as well. Paris–Roubaix? Milan–San Remo? Lombardy? We're talking 10 minutes to a quarter of an hour. That's how Fausto Coppi was.

Sadness and scandal also affected Coppi's career. The war consumed what would undoubtedly have been some of his greatest years. His brother, also a racer, died after crashing at the climax of the Giro del Piemonte, when his wheel caught in rails of the Turin tram. Italy was also scandalised after the married Coppi started an affair with a married woman (a crime in Italy at the time). And finally, he died tragically young, aged only 40, of malaria contracted in Africa after an exhibition race. Despite the sadness that dogged his career, Coppi remains one of the most successful, talented and elegant riders of all time.

Above Stage 18, Bagneres de Bogirre to Pau – Fausto Coppi leads the way on the Tour of 1952.

Right Victorious! Fausto Coppi wins the Tour of 1952.

COPPI'S NOTABLE WINS

Giro d'Italia:

★★★★★

(between 1940 and 1953)

Tour de France:

★★

(1949 and 1952)

World Championships:

★

(1953)

Probably the most brilliant and brutally competitive of all champions has to be Eddy Merckx. He ended his eighteen-year career with 525 victories to his name, including 11 Grand Tour victories (Vuelta, Giro, Tour). Merckx was born in Belgium in 1945, a grocer's son. He was good at all sports, including basketball, table tennis, football – and significantly for this ultra-competitive sportsman – boxing. However, he rode a bike from the age of four and said that he wanted to be a racing cyclist from that age 'when I listened to the Tour de France on the radio'. He got his racing licence at sixteen and never looked back. He gained the nickname 'the Cannibal', so remorseless was his desire to win. He would think nothing of mounting an attack with 100 km of a race to go. He simply gave it his all: after races he needed a chair in the shower because he didn't have the strength to stand up.

For much of the time his dominance was seen by some as damaging the sport. But the French writer Pierre Chany commented: 'has anyone wondered whether Molière damaged theatre ... Bach harmed music?'

18 year career, in which he achieved

525 victories including

11 Grand Tour victories (Vuelta, Giro, Tour)

At a velodrome race in Blois in 1969 Merckx collided with his pacer. The pacer was killed and Merckx suffered serious head injuries, and twisted his spine and pelvis. 'From that day', according to Merckx, 'cycling became suffering'. He tried various methods to alleviate the sciatic pain that plagued him from then on, constantly adjusting his saddle and riding position, even sleeping with a wooden board under his bed. He won the 1970 Tour, but the winning was becoming more difficult. In 1971 Luis Ocana was ahead by 11 minutes, before crashing in the 14th stage and leaving the race, allowing Merckx to go on to win. Merckx kept competing, however, and kept on winning. He retired in 1978, but competed to the end, saying that 'without the crash I could have won more Tours'. Perhaps Merckx is the best person to sum up his own attitude towards the sport: 'The day when I start a race without intending to win it, I won't be able to look at myself in the mirror'.

Left Eddy Merckx takes to the mountains on the Tour of 1969.

Right Merckx wins the Milan – San Remo of 1971. The longest one day race at 298 km, Merckx went on to win it seven times.

BIKES IN BOOKS

In 1898, H.G. Wells published 'The Time Machine', perhaps the most important and influential of all science fiction novels. It features a late nineteenth century gentleman scientist who travels into the future to discover the eventual fate of the human race. But what at first looks like paradise, a land of leisure and plenty, soon reveals its dystopian underside. The Time Traveller realises that the human race has split into two races – the Eloi, a weak, childlike species, and the Morlocks, a subterranean underclass that uses them for food. In a clever re-envisioning of Darwin, Wells suggests that the bourgeois comforts of modern times will eventually emasculate mankind, and that the divisions of middle class and working class will widen irreconcilably.

Although the novel owes its intellectual inspiration to nineteenth-century evolutionary theory, *The Time Machine* itself owes much to the bicycle. The Time Traveller straddles it like a bike. And like a keen amateur cyclist, he gives it a routine check before setting off – 'a last tap, tried all the screws again, put one more drop of oil on the quartz rod, and sat myself in the saddle'. And as he goes 'reeling' into the future, Wells pictures his traveller almost as an early cyclist out of control:

...this time I was not seated properly in the saddle, but sideways and in an unstable fashion. For an indefinite time I clung to the machine as it swayed and vibrated, quite unheeding how I went ...

Wells was an enthusiastic cyclist. His earlier novel, *The Wheels of Chance: A Bicycling Idyll* (1896), is filled with a sense of the wonder of the cycling boom of the 1890s, as Mr Hoopdriver the draper goes on a tour of the South of England.

On his way he meets a young woman, Jesse Milton, also a cyclist. Jesse is escaping her suburban origins and in doing so wears 'rationals' - trousers tucked into stockings. Just as cycling offers Hoopdriver a new form of social mobility, the natural demands of cycling thus suggests a new freedom for women and the blurring of gender roles. However, this doesn't necessarily have a positive outcome. Despite Hoopdriver chivalrously rescuing Jesse from the attentions of the bounder Behamel, Jesse returns home, determined to 'Live her Own Life'. Hoopdriver, disillusioned, returns to the drapery counter. For Wells, bicycling represents an opportunity missed: that of class reconciliation, the consequences of this failure being the false idyll of the *Time Machine*. In his autobiography, published in 1934, Wells looks back sentimentally, to a time when 'the bicycle was the swiftest thing upon the roads... there were as yet no automobiles and the cyclist had a lordliness, a sense of masterful adventure, that has gone from him altogether now'.

Bikes have always attracted writers for similar reasons - representing romantic escape, but also standing at the hinge of the natural and the mechanical worlds. There is therefore something quintessentially comic about bicycles: clowns go round on unicycles, monkeys ride bikes. For the Irish writer Samuel Beckett, bicycling embodies the philosopher Descartes' view of the human: of the body as a machine, and the mind as a rider. But whereas Descartes viewed them as fitting together neatly, for Beckett, cycling shows how inefficient, and cumbersome the fit is - as seen in how the hero of *Molloy* attempts to straddle his mount:

I fastened my crutches to the cross-bar, one on either side, I propped the foot of my stiff leg (I forget which, now they're both stiff) on the projecting front axle, and I pedalled with the other.

Above Far from the madding crowd – Thomas Hardy, writer and cyclist, at his home in Max Gate, Dorset in the 1920s.

Far left To infinity and beyond – a still from the film of *The Time Machine* (1960).

Enid Blyton, who did much to immortalise cycling in her Famous Five books, presents a Raleigh to a child at a Road Safety Competition in 1949.

On the other hand, Flann O'Brien's comic masterpiece, *The Third Policeman*, contains a local policeman who expounds his 'Atomic Theory' whereby humans are turning into bikes and vice versa:

> *"The gross and net result of it is that people who spend most of their natural lives riding iron bicycles over the rocky roadsteads of this parish get their personalities mixed up with the personalities of their bicycle as a result of the interchanging of the atoms of each of them, and you would be surprised at the number of people in these parts who nearly are half people and half bicycles."*

I let go a gasp of astonishment that made a sound in the air like a bad puncture.

"And you would be flabbergasted at the number of bicycles that are half human, almost half man, half partaking of humanity."

The Policeman explains how the local postman is 71 per cent bicycle, as a result of doing a 38-mile delivery round for 40 years. The novel climaxes in a scene of bicycle sex as the narrator sets off down the road, his leg muscles pumping:

How can I convey the perfection of my comfort on the bicycle, the completeness of my union with her, the sweet responses she gave me at every particle of her frame? [...] She moved beneath me with agile sympathy in a swift, airy stride, finding smooth ways among the stony tracks, swaying and bending skilfully to match my changing attitudes, even accommodating her left pedal patiently to the awkward working of my wooden leg.

For O'Brien, unlike Descartes and Beckett, the human and the mechanical merge with the clickety joyousness of well-adjusted index shifting.

OTHER BICYCLE BOOKS OF NOTE

- **The Rider by Tim Krabbé** A surreal Dutch novel showing a rider's eye view of Tour de Mont Aigoual in southern France.

- **Cat by Freya North** About a woman journalist covering the Tour de France.

- **The Adventure of the Priory School by Arthur Conan Doyle** Sherlock Holmes is brought in to solve a kidnapping mystery where a great deal hangs on the difference between two sets of cycle tyre tracks.

- **Three Men on the Bummel (also known as Three Men on Wheels),** from that English master of comic prose, Jerome K. Jerome and his sequel to *Three Men in a Boat*. 'Bummel' is a German word, which the narrator explains means 'a journey, long or short, without an end; the only thing regulating it being the necessity of getting back within a given time to the point from which one started.' On a tour of the Black Forest in Germany, three friends capture the earnest aimlessness that is the pleasure of cycling.

THE VELODROME

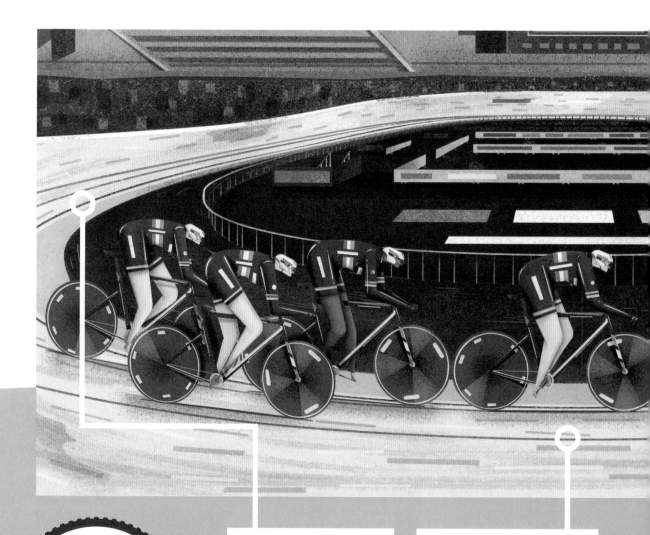

There are a lot of markings on the standard track but three lines are particularly important (other than the finish line!). These all run right round the track.

MEASURING LINE

Black, if track is a light colour, or white if it's dark. This runs 20 cm from the track's inside edge and marks exactly the 250 metre distance.

STAYER'S LINE

Marked in blue at a third of the width of the track, or 2.45 metres from the track's inner edge, whichever is the greater. This is a separation line in the madison races for the resting riders.

Track cycling provides a more homogenous environment for competitive cycling than the road. It allows for a large variety of events, all of which rely on the cyclist having a sprinter's explosive speed, often allied with a chess player's cunning. While you can have velodromes of pretty much any size, in order to comply with UCI regulations there are some restrictions, and these are even more stringent when it comes to Olympic and World Championship competitions. In essence, though, a velodrome generally consists of two straights linked at either end by a banked curve. This basic construction enables the riders to reach incredible speeds and provides a fabulous setting for watching race riding.

For the Olympics and World Championships the length of the track must be 250 metres and its width must be constant all the way around. There are no set regulations regarding the height of the banking other than that the transition to the straight should be gradual.

There are an innumerable number of ways to skin the proverbial cat and there are almost as many ways to race around the 250 metre oval – most can either be raced individually or as a team event.

SPRINT Almost the most basic of all races. Over three laps the quickest cyclist wins... but it is not quite that simple. Races are decided on a best of three and because 750 metres is a fair old distance to just sprint from a standing start a lot of 'cat and mouse' has developed in these races. Neither rider wants to take the lead too early so they will manoeuvre to try to force the other to take the lead. It's generally not until the final lap that the speed is injected. For the team version the race is over three laps for men (with three riders) and two for women (with two riders). The competing teams start on either straight and each rider must lead his team for one lap.

TIME TRIAL This is the most basic race, with just one rider at once on the track, and the quickest time wins. It is competed over 200 metres (with a flying start, usually only as a qualifying discipline for the longer distance event), 500 metres (women), 1,000 metres (men).

SPRINTER'S LINE

Marked in red, 65 cm in from the measuring line, this is the ideal racing line around the track.

PURSUIT The competing cyclists start on opposite straights and race over a fixed distance. If either cyclist catches the other the race is over but if neither is caught the winner is the one who completes the set distance in the quickest time. Perversely in spite of its name this is, in effect, a sprint but without the 'cat and mouse' element. The team event is exactly the same and is competed by teams of four riders.

POINTS RACE Riders compete over distances up to 40 km for points won in sprints during the race. On 250 metre tracks there is a sprint every 10 laps. The winner of each sprint gains 5 points, second wins 3, third 2 and fourth 1. Points can also be gained and lost by gaining or losing a lap on the field. 20 points up or down in each case. To gain a lap a rider has to get away from the group and catch up with the rear of the largest group. A rider loses a lap when he drops behind and is caught by the leading group.

KEIRIN This is a sprint race with between 5 and 7 riders. The cyclists follow behind a pacing motorbike which slowly increases its speed up to 50 kph (31 mph), reaching this speed with about a kilometre to the finish and departing the track with around 600-700 metres remaining. It is then a straight sprint to the finish.

MADISON Teams of two compete over distances up to 50 km aiming to win points in sprints. The points are the same as for the points race. The main difference in the Madison is that only one rider is actually racing at any one time and may tag in his or her team mate and even give them a slingshot start by pulling them forward. The race takes its name from New York's famous sporting arena, Madison Square Garden.

SIX DAY RACES The original six day races were purely a test of one man's endurance; who could ride the furthest over the allotted time. Teams of two were then introduced so that one rider could rest while the other rode. The races can also incorporate time trials, sprints and eliminations.

Right Baseball legend Joe DiMaggio fires a pistol to start the spring 1939 six-day race at Madison Square Garden, New York.

Below The rider on the motorbike always wins!

SCRATCH This is a straight race but over longer distances. For Elite men it is 15 km and women 10 km. Any rider lapped by the main bunch has to leave the race.

ELIMINATION Over a pre-set distance, dependent on the number of competitors, a sprint is run every two laps. The last rider to cross the finishing line in each sprint is eliminated from the race. This continues until the final two riders compete the final sprint. It was originally known as *Devil Takes the Hindmost*.

OMNIUM This takes its name from the Latin, which translates as 'all' and therefore comprises pretty much everything above. It is the equivalent of the heptathlon or decathlon in athletics and is competed over two days. The races included are: Scratch, Pursuit, Elimination, Time Trial, Flying Lap and Points Race.

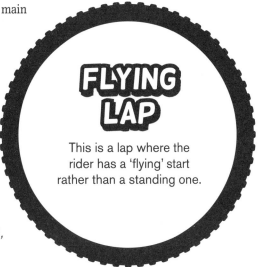

FLYING LAP

This is a lap where the rider has a 'flying' start rather than a standing one.

SCIENCE AND TECHNOLOGY

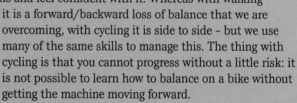

BALANCE EINSTEIN-A-GO-GO

How often have you heard someone say 'it's just like riding a bike'? Have you ever thought what that cliché means? Generally what it means is that once you've learnt how to do something you will never forget. As far as bicycle riding goes it is actually not so much a case of learning something new, as adapting what you already know and do to new circumstances.

As babies we learn how to stand, balance and walk and if you think about those skills, the simple act of walking, you'll realise that all you are doing is losing your balance and regaining it. Every step is a controlled forward fall from one leg that is arrested by your other leg coming forward, and so on. You never actually feel like you're falling though.

Cycling is all about balance, or at least basic cycling is, and you can't progress until you can achieve this and feel confident with it. Whereas with walking

it is a forward/backward loss of balance that we are overcoming, with cycling it is side to side – but we use many of the same skills to manage this. The thing with cycling is that you cannot progress without a little risk: it is not possible to learn how to balance on a bike without getting the machine moving forward.

Before we move on we need to understand what balance actually is. It's something we take for granted and rarely think about but it's worth taking a moment. An object is in balance when the line of gravity is held inside the supporting base of the object. For a pyramid, for example, the line of gravity runs straight down from the point to the centre of the base. For a person, when they are standing up straight it goes from the top of their head to a point on the ground in between their feet. Sitting on a bike it runs, again, from the top of the rider's head down to a line running between the wheels. If the line of gravity moves too far either side of this the result is inevitable – you'll fall off.

Going back to what we said before, you need to move the bike forward to have any chance of balancing, so risk is involved. (It is possible to balance with the bike stationary, it's called a track stand, but that's for the pros or people who think they are pros and want to show off at traffic lights.) In order to balance we have to take in and process a lot of information. This comes from two main sources: our eyes and our ears. The first of these is obvious: you can see if you're balancing by looking at the surrounding area and making sure you are upright in relation to it. The second, the ears, is not an audio sense, but is part of the deep structure of the inner ear called the vestibular system. It is the movement of fluids within this part of the ear that help us to balance.

There is also a direct link between the vestibular system and vision. If you turn your head to one side while looking forward, you'll notice that your eyes move to keep looking ahead. You don't consciously do this, it's the interaction between the vestibular system and your eyes. The same happens when you look up and down.

If you close your eyes and lie down you know you're horizontal thanks to your inner ear. Experience also comes into this, and muscle memory. This is the final element to keeping you balanced. Your muscles take in information constantly about the strains and pressure on them and make tiny continuous adjustments to keep you upright. This is as much the case for walking as being on a bike.

The added complication of cycling is that, unlike a pyramid, you and your bike are not making a naturally stable object. By being on the bike your centre of gravity is raised further from the ground, and this makes balance harder. By the bike having two wheels in line with each other, balancing is harder. Think of a tricycle – it's totally stable and requires no effort to balance, but if you started to move the two rear wheels closer together you'd eventually reach a point where the rider would need to balance the machine. Taking all of this into account, the important question is how does the cyclist actually stay upright? The answer, on paper, is simple, but in practice takes a lot of practise. Balance is achieved through small changes in the steering and your body's position.

Let's take the steering first. If the bike is falling to the left, in order to regain balance you need to steer to the left. This brings the centre of gravity back towards the support base. It is this that makes it quite difficult when first learning because what you need to do is to steer towards the fall, when your natural instinct is to steer away from it. The amazing thing is that if you push a bicycle along, with no rider, it does this for itself. Try it, it's amazing. Adjusting your body position is a little more complicated and will only work for small losses of balance. By shifting your body position you are moving the centre of gravity and, hopefully, the bike will follow. It's a combination of these two things in conjunction with the forward motion that you keep you upright. Unless, of course, you've mastered that track stand.

A trick cyclist from the early 1900s makes defying gravity look very easy.

AERODYNAMICS
SHAVING OFF THE SECONDS

Most of a cyclist's energy is expended in simply pushing him or herself and the bike through the air. Statistics vary but it takes somewhere around 80 per cent of a cyclist's effort just to force through the air. Wind resistance is a cyclist's greatest enemy, which explains why so much time, effort and money has been spent on reducing the effects of this speed-killing muscle sapper. It should actually be called air resistance because calling it wind resistance might lead one to think that it doesn't exist on a non-windy day. The important thing to note is that there are many elements that go towards creating air resistance, and even as a cyclist commuting to work it is possible to reduce some of them with very simple changes. Competing with Chris Hoy, however, is another matter altogether.

With all of the following the thing to bear in mind is that air resistance is at its least destructive when it is presented with the smallest, smoothest surface. So a snooker ball is much less affected by wind resistance than a pine cone.

Bikes with flat frames and discs for wheels rather than spokes offer least air resistance.

Rider's Position

Most people cycling to work will be on a standard upright bicycle, sitting pretty much straight up. This is a comfortable position and allows the rider to see above traffic, for the most part, and no one wants to beat any world records on the way to their 9 to 5. The problem is that this position presents a large flat surface to the air – your chest – which creates

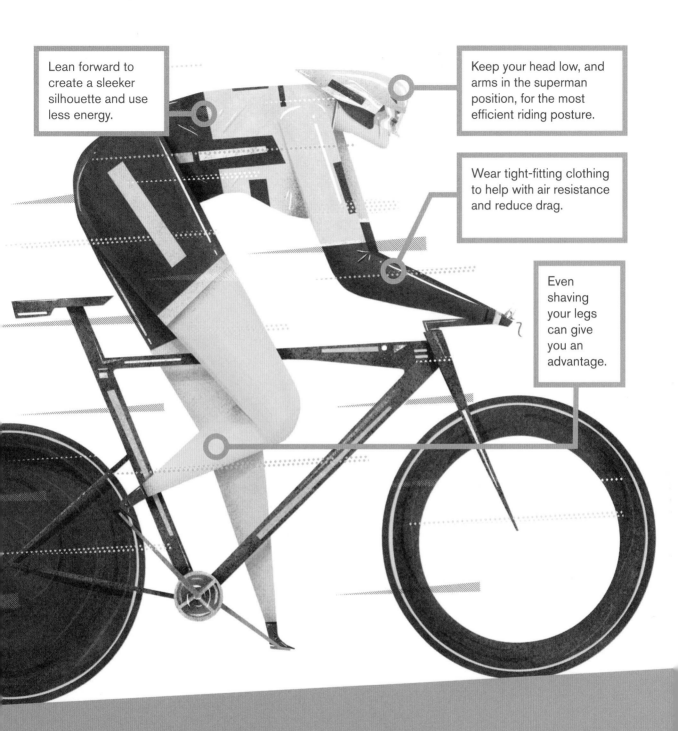

Lean forward to create a sleeker silhouette and use less energy.

Keep your head low, and arms in the superman position, for the most efficient riding posture.

Wear tight-fitting clothing to help with air resistance and reduce drag.

Even shaving your legs can give you an advantage.

a huge amount of resistance. Even leaning forward just a little will reduce this, and the more you lean forward the less resistance there is. Remember it will mean that not only can you go quicker but you'll also use less energy doing so.

The most efficient position on a standard bike, if you have the right handlebars to do it, is the superman, with both arms out ahead and the body leaning fully forward, with the head low. It's not really practical for riding to work but gives you an idea of what you're aiming for. The other alternative is the recumbent bicycle, where the cyclist is actually lying down, with their feet out in front. It presents a smaller area to the air and is quite aerodynamic.

The Peloton Effect

It's well known that the peloton in a big road race can travel much quicker than a lone rider, and even on a daily commute it is possible to take advantage of this. This is called drafting or slipstreaming and even cycling closely behind a fellow cyclist will give you some clear air through which to travel. It has even been discovered that the rider in front receives a benefit from this by being pushed from behind!

Clothing

It's obvious when you watch any professional cyclist that tight clothing is an advantage in getting through the air. For the average commute just wearing a well fitting coat, as opposed to a loose one, can make up to 10 per cent difference in the amount of drag. Cycle clips don't only stop your trousers getting caught in the chain, they also reduce resistance by presenting a smaller surface area to the onrushing air.

The main function of a helmet is of course safety but it can also reduce air resistance. It keeps your hair under control, no bad thing for that journey to the office, and presents a smooth surface for the air to flow over.

Luggage

Carrying panniers or bags is bound to create more air resistance so making sure they are tightly packed is important. Many people now use covers not only to keep them dry, but also to produce a smoother surface over which the air can travel.

Hair

Shaving the hair off your legs, if you are brave enough, and it's warm enough to cycle in shorts, can reduce the drag by over 5 per cent. It may not be everyone's aesthetic choice but it could get you to your destination feeling that little bit less tired. The drag of a beard depends very much on your body position but it too can slow you down.

Above Riding in a peloton gives benefits to all the members right to the back.
Right The aim is to present as small an area as possible to the on-rushing air.

The Bike

There are a number of elements of the bike itself that get in the way of the air. Modern racing frames do not use round tubing as it causes air resistance; they mainly use flat frames. The wheels are often made of discs rather than with spokes. Even the spokes cause wind resistance, but because disc wheels are heavier you won't see them used in road racing, the advantage is too small to justify the extra weight over such long distances.

A final thing to ponder is that the speed you are travelling will have a large effect on the air resistance that you encounter. What you are doing when you are cycling, or moving at all, is shifting your bulk through air molecules. When you move slowly you actually meet very little air resistance and it is only as you start to accelerate and reach higher speeds, above about 10 mph (16 kph), that air resistance kicks in. It's difficult to actually feel this change but think about walking in a swimming pool. At low speeds you can walk almost normally but when you try to run the water really gets in the way and slows you down. The quicker you try to run the harder it is and it is exactly the same when cycling; the quicker you cycle the more air resistance has an effect on you. It is not just that you are colliding with the air more quickly, but also that you are colliding with more air over a shorter period of time.

THE HOUR
IT'S ONLY 3,600 SECONDS

The nature of being human is to push ourselves to our limits. It is this drive that has seen mankind reach the moon, climb to the top of the Everest and eat 271 baked beans in five minutes using just a cocktail stick. Whatever the arena we want to push the margins, and cycling is no different. The Hour record is one way in which cyclists have tested themselves against each other, and the clock, ever since the first chain turned a link.

Actually, it was even before the introduction of the chain and the Safety Bicycle that the first hour record was set by James Moore of Wolverhampton. It was in the bicycle grounds of the Molineux Hotel, where the famous Wolverhampton Wanderers later played football, that Moore laid down the first mark. Riding a Penny Farthing, Moore cycled 14 miles 880 yards (23.33 km) in 60 minutes in 1873, four years after winning the first cycle road race from Paris to Rouen.

With the founding of the International Cycling Association (ICA) in 1892, the first record to be officially sanctioned was in 1893 when Henri Desgrange covered 21.95 miles (35.33 km) in Paris' Buffalo Velodrome. Desgrange is of course better known as the organiser of the first Tour de France. It's worth noting that towards the end of the nineteenth and the start of the twentieth century, greater speeds were set, but have never been included in the official records by the ICA or its successor the UCI. This is because they were achieved by professional cyclists. How times change!

Up until just after the start of the First World War there was a ding-dong battle for the record between the Swiss rider Oscar Egg and the Frenchman Marcel Berthet. The Hour changed hands several times between them over a two-year period up to 18 August 1914 when Egg scrambled over the line to set a mark of 27.49 miles (44.25 km) which would stand for 19 years.

Sir Bradley Wiggins set a new hour record (33.88 miles/ 54.526 km) on 7 June 2015.

It was a Dutchman, Jan van Hout, who took up the baton in 1933 when he increased the record by just 341 metres. Sadly van Hout was a victim of the German concentration camps and died in Neuengamme in 1945. After the French rider Maurice Richard beat van Hout's mark just a month after the Dutchman had set it, The Hour, in effect, moved to Italy for thirty years. Not because it was held for all that time by an Italian but because the next ten records were set at the Vigorelli Velodrome in Milan.

In the year it was opened, 1935, the stadium saw its first hour record when Giuseppe Olmo became the first rider to break the 45 kilometre barrier. When Richard took the record back a year later the track's reputation for being the fastest in the world was established. By the time the stadium hosted The Beatles in 1965 its place in the record books was almost over, with Jacques Anquetil's record-breaking ride in 1967 not being allowed by the UCI due to his refusal to attend a drugs test.

When Danish professional, Ole Ritter set a new mark of 30.23 miles (48.65 km) in Mexico City in 1968, just ahead of the Olympic Games, The Hour was about to enter something of a twilight zone thanks to the advances in technology which went hand in hand with leaps forward in technique. Eddy Merckx knocked Ritter off the perch in 1972, again in Mexico City, when he added

778 metres to the record. This record would stand for 12 years and it is here that things got quicker, but also rather confusing for anyone trying to keep track of things, yet Merckx's record, although no one knew it at the time, would draw a very deep line in the sand.

In January 1984, Francesco Moser, just a few months away from winning his only grand tour, the Giro d'Italia, rolled on to the concrete track of Agustin Melgar, which had staged the track cycling events at the 1968 Mexico Olympics. Wearing a skinsuit and riding a bike with disc wheels, Moser broke the 50 km barrier on 19 January – but that proved to be just a practice run when four days later he broke the 51 km mark. By pushing the record up by 1,720 metres, the greatest leap since the end of the previous century, Moser sent shockwaves through the sport. But governing bodies are like oil tankers and they take a long time to turn.

Before the 'tanker' turned there was time in the early 1990s for two British cyclists to push The Hour even further. Graeme Obree and Chris Boardman were both fantastic cyclists, but both were also driven to push their bikes to the limits of engineering. Obree in his own workshop, and Boardman with the expertise of Lotus cars, created futuristic bikes that allowed them to improve further on Moser's mark. By the time they had finished their personal battle in September 1996, Boardman had improved the standard to an astonishing 35.03 miles (56.375 km). Their bikes looked almost nothing like that used by Merckx and their riding position, the superman invented by Obree, was also a world away from that of the Belgian. And so it was in 1997 that the UCI split the hour into two, one the official Hour record, the other referred to as the Best Human Effort (BHE). The UCI decreed that Hour record attempts could only be made on equipment that was equivalent to that used by Merckx, while for the BHE the gloves, in effect, were taken off.

Sadly, in the same way that having too many sanctioning bodies has reduced the interest in boxing, this split had the effect of diminishing the allure of The Hour. The desire was still there to hold the record but which record? You might beat Merckx but still come nowhere near Boardman's BHE. It was somewhat fitting then that the first rider to beat Merckx's record under the new ruling was Chris Boardman. He did so in 2000 when he added 10 metres to the record. The fact that this was 28 years after Merckx set his mark shows how amazing the Belgian's ride had been.

Five years later Ondrej Sosenka added a further 259 metres to the record and, in effect, he still holds the record because the UCI turned again in 2014 and re-unified The Hour! In a slightly strange ruling they scrapped the BHE as a mark, reinstated Obree and Boardman's previously illegal rides into the record books but set the new record at Sosenka's distance, even though it was shorter than those of the two Brits. While this rule change left many scratching their heads it did re-ignite interest in the record. It became simple once again with one target to beat and one hour to do it.

In the short time since the rule change the record has been increased five times. The German Jens Voigt was the first to do it, adding 1,400 metres to the mark in September 2014 in his final ride. Matthias Brändle moved it on again a month later but only held the record for four months before the Australian Rohan Dennis reached 32.62 miles (52.49 km). Alex Dowsett brought the record back to Britain where it all began by setting 32.9 miles (52.937 km) on 2 May 2015, but his glory was short-lived.

When Sir Bradley Wiggins announced he was to attempt the record few doubted he would do it. His career has never skirted with failure and he is known as one of the best time-trial riders in the history of the sport. What no one expected was that he would add such a great distance to Dowsett's record. On 7 June 2015, Wiggins cycled around the Lee Valley Velodrome, best known for hosting the cycling at the 2012 London Olympics, for 3,600 seconds. In that time he went around the 250 metre track just over 218 times to set a new Hour record of 33.88 miles (54.526 km). He'd beaten Dowsett by over 1.5 km. This amazing effort made sure that The Hour was back where it belonged and means that anyone who tries to beat it will truly have the toughest ride of their life.

FITNESS
IT'S NOT ONLY ABOUT THE BIKE

If it was all about the bike we could all win the Tour de France, given the correct machine. One of the criticisms of motor-racing's Formula One is that the best car wins and you could put almost any of the top 20 drivers in it and it would still win. However, this is not the case for cycling, so it's important to have a look at how to make sure you are cycle-ready.

For someone who pootles along on their bike for weekend outings or to get to work there is very little you need to do to make your cycling life better. The main thing at this level is not to push yourself too far beyond your limits. You don't want to get to work feeling too tired but you do want to enjoy the ride. Make sure you eat a good light breakfast. Doing exercise, any exercise, in the morning without breakfast is a recipe, excuse the pun, for disaster. Even cycling slowly you'll be burning up more calories than driving or travelling on the bus and if you haven't got those calories to burn you'll get tired more quickly. Cereal and fruit are both good, coffee isn't bad. You just need to put some petrol in the tank.

You'll find that regular cycling such as a work commute improves your fitness all by itself. Without busting a gut it's a good idea to use the journey to push yourself a little harder. Everyone wants to get home as soon as possible after a hard day's work, so why not try to get home in less time than it took you to get to work? Stay safe, of course, but just push yourself a little and gradually you'll get stronger and you'll find that your morning commute speeds up, too.

Left Even in the 1930s, Rudge-Whitworth were keen to show your cycle could be used for travel to the office while boosting your health.

Right Hydration is vital. Here Fiorenzo Magni takes it to extremes during the 1950 Tour de France.

It might seem obvious but one of the best ways to get fit for cycling is to cycle! Clearly it uses all the muscles that you need and tests your ability in similar ways, but you need to be strategic in how you use your cycling to improve your fitness for cycling. If you are planning to compete, or if you just want to travel a little faster, it's useful to push yourself but do it smartly. The legs are the most important part of your body's equipment for cycling and a quick and easy way to build up their strength and endurance is to cycle standing up. You'll be surprised how quickly this tires you out when you first try it but it's only when muscles get fatigued that they can grow. Don't go crazy with it but when you start, on any journey, alternate between a long sit and a short stand. Start off with just five seconds every minute and slowly over the course of a few weeks increase that to twenty seconds standing and forty sitting. The good thing with this exercise

During the 1966 Giro, Vittorio Adorni, Gianni Motta and Jacques Anquetil replenish their carbs by enjoying a plate of spaghetti.

is that it also increases your core strength, you'll feel your stomach muscles straining, and it improves your general control of the bike.

This sort of interval training is used by the pros and another such exercise involves hills. It depends where you live of course, but try to find a gentle slope to start with, maybe a 1 in 25 gradient. Pick a gear for the uphill that is just outside your comfort zone. Again, fitness only improves if you push the limits but you don't need to push too far. Little by little is the best way. Cycle up the hill and then use the downhill to rest. If you find the uphill too easy go up a gear, but it should only be just a little uncomfortable. The next time you come back to this hill you'll probably find that the gear which was uncomfortable last time is now in your comfort zone. You can combine the above two exercises. Once a gear is in your comfort zone on the uphill, rather than go up a gear, stay in the same gear but cycle standing up.

It's not necessary to do the above exercises in a totally structured way. You can incorporate them into your usual cycle route. You know where the hills are and where the good places to rest are so just plan ahead and you can turn any regular ride or commute into a training session. If you are doing this on the way to the office though it's a good idea to take a change of clothes!

One of the problems with exercising on your bike on the road is that you will often have to stop mid-workout for annoying things like traffic lights, so it is worth using an exercise bike every now and then to have uninterrupted sessions. Bikes in gyms don't offer the wind resistance you get in the real world but do give the chance to finely tune the work you do without the random intrusions you get on the road. As with all exercise, it's a good idea to set yourself targets, making them achievable but not too easy. You can replicate all of the work described above on most machines and because of the stats provided it is simple to compare your performance over time and make sure that you are improving.

If you're in the gym anyway have a look at the other machines and think about the muscles you are using when cycling and how those machines can help you. Most of these are obvious but one area that is often forgotten is the arms. Depending on your cycling style the arms can take a big load and quite a battering so it's essential to make sure you keep them strong and flexible.

As with most sport the most important part of the body you'll use is between your ears. Cycling on the road can be dangerous and you need to concentrate at all times to mitigate these dangers. This means you should try to avoid cycling when you're over-tired, distracted or stressed. Also use your brain to monitor your cycling, making sure that you are using your equipment, your body that is, as efficiently as possible, and that your cycling position is right.

A final thing to consider is that every now and then it is good to take a break from your bike. It might be rainy or you might be too busy for a cycle ride and you need to allow yourself to put the bicycle clips away for a day. Getting the bus or train is not failure and it's a well known fact that for muscles to grow they need time off every now then, so think of rest days as part of your fitness regime not an escape from it.

This pile-up happened in
the 1979 Tour, proving that
even the professionals fall off
sometimes.

WIPEOUT!
FALLING OFF SAFELY

Anyone who has ever straddled a bicycle has had that moment when it all went wrong and they found themselves on the ground rather than in the saddle. From Anquetil to Zoetemelk everyone has had the discomfort of having his or her fall broken by the hard cold road – but it doesn't always have to end in a trip to the hospital. While all falls are potentially dangerous there are some things you can do to prepare yourself and try to reduce the possibility of serious injury.

This is obvious but it's worth remembering that the best way to avoid injury from a fall or crash is to avoid the accident in the first place. Most of the time falls can't be avoided, but it is sadly true that some are caused by cyclists themselves. The roads are getting busier every year with more cars, lorries, buses and, yes, bikes, so it is important to think ahead. If you can anticipate danger you have a much better chance of avoiding it. Some basic things to avoid are racing up the inside of stationary traffic, vehicles in the approach to junctions (finding a gap between them is safest), and trying to beat the lights or the person approaching a pedestrian crossing.

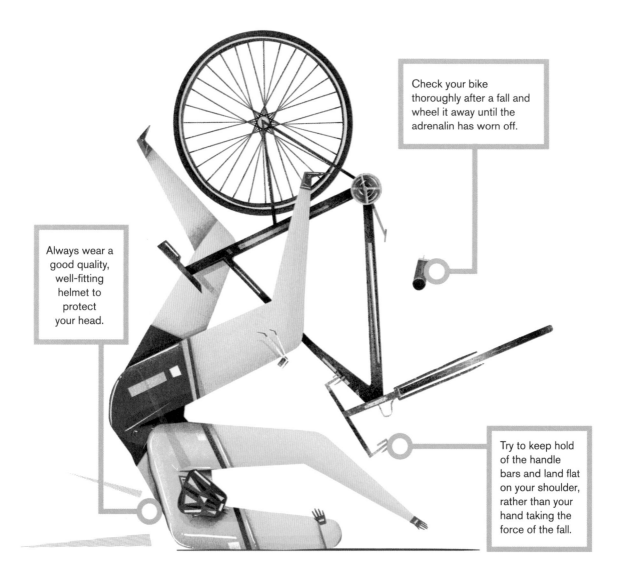

Check your bike thoroughly after a fall and wheel it away until the adrenalin has worn off.

Always wear a good quality, well-fitting helmet to protect your head.

Try to keep hold of the handle bars and land flat on your shoulder, rather than your hand taking the force of the fall.

No matter how safely you cycle, or plan ahead, or avoid busy routes, there will probably come a time when you take a tumble. The first thing to do, right now, is buy a good, well-fitting helmet. There is an argument against helmets that says car drivers are more careful around cyclists without them. The counter-argument is that most car drivers do not take sufficient notice of cyclists to see what they are wearing, so buy that helmet.

Interestingly it is often in the quicker crashes that injuries are less serious. In a crash that happens quickly you don't have time to put your arm out to break your fall so you're still holding on to the handlebars when you hit the road. What this means is that you are, almost by total accident, in a better position to avoid injury. Most experts agree that by keeping a tight compact shape you'll avoid major breaks.

The most common injuries when falling are broken collar, hand and wrist bones. It is a natural reaction, even among the pros, to put your hand out when you fall. We've done it since childhood and sometimes instinct just takes over.

Above Taking a tumble and how to minimise the risk of injury.

The problem is that if you fall off your bike and try to break that fall with your outstretched hand the most likely thing to happen is a break somewhere along that limb. When your hand hits the ground the full force of the fall goes straight into it and up your arm. If your hand or wrist don't break the most likely fracture is your collar bone, it's the last place the force will hit and that energy has to go somewhere. Getting into a ball-like shape, with elbows and knees tucked in and head down is the best way to avoid major bone fractures.

The problem with the ball-shape approach is that it just doesn't feel natural. The natural thing to do is to let go of the bike and put your hand out. So what should you do if you find instinct taking over? The most important thing is to try to absorb the impact by allowing your outstretched arm to bend. If it's locked straight you will almost certainly get a break somewhere but if it's just slightly bent when you hit the deck you can take some of the strain away by letting the arm bend thus helping you to roll.

If you can keep hold of the handlebars you will naturally stop your hand going out, and with your head down it will also keep your shoulders rounded meaning that when you fall you are more likely to land on the flat of your shoulder. This is a larger area than a hand, elbow or shoulder point, and the impact is dissipated across this larger area. It may look brutal but often a skid along the road will result in a bit more blood but less long-term injury. If you're sliding along the surface it means you're not hitting the road head on.

Another thing to consider is where you land. Falling into a grass verge is going to be a lot less painful than falling into the road, and it is also further away from any other traffic. Again this is as much to do with anticipation as preparation. It's impossible to *plan* where your next accident will happen but it is useful to ponder it. Where on your route are the major trouble spots? Are there safer routes to go, or do you need to make sure you're more on your game at certain points? The shortest route is not always the quickest nor the safest.

Whenever we fall, not just on bikes, our natural instinct is to try to jump straight back up. Obviously if you have fallen in the middle of the road with traffic you need to get out of the way but once you're in a safe place give yourself time to assess the damage. If your head has taken any sort of knock it is a good idea to get to A&E or call an ambulance. If you're sure your head didn't take a hit check everything else out. Are all your joints able to move without pain, have you got any cuts or friction burns? It's worth checking under your clothes because sometimes, due to the adrenalin rush, you may not feel the pain but you may have cuts that have not bled through your clothes but need treatment. If you feel okay to carry on you need to check your bike before you do so. All the usual things - brakes, wheels, chain, lights and so on. Even if everything seems ok it can often be better, if practical, to lock your bike up and finish the journey on public transport or just wheel the bike and walk. Sometimes the after-effects of a crash won't become apparent until your muscles have cooled down.

As already stated the best thing to do is never fall off your bike, but unfortunately life isn't that simple. All you can do is be prepared, stay aware and try to stay safe.

RECYCLE AND REVOLUTION

THE REINVENTION
FOLDING BIKES

One of the best-loved films of all time is 'Chitty Chitty Bang Bang', the tale of a written-off racing car that is brought back to life by eccentric inventor, and single father, Caractacus Potts. Through the car his children find happiness, and Potts (played by Dick Van Dyke) finds a wife in the shape of Truly Scrumptious (Sally Ann Howes).

But part of the joy of the film comes from the inventions that clutter the Potts household, built by the English artist and cartoonist, Rowland Emett. There is a breakfast making machine, a portable automatic barber shop, and a little dragon carpet sweeper – which devours rugs as well as dust. The brilliance of Emett's inventions lies in their use of everyday objects – a whisk, a lampshade, a badminton racket. But central to his whole aesthetic is the bicycle: wheels and chains provide the power; sausages stick to wheel rims; and in perhaps his greatest invention – 'The Featherstone Kite Openwork Basketweave Gentleman's MK2 Flying Machine' – an Edwardian gentleman uses only bicycle bits and an umbrella to take off.

Inventors have always loved bicycles. What could be better proof of one's inventiveness than reinventing one of the best inventions ever made? Over the course of the century bicycles have therefore been continually tweaked and twisted, transformed, customised and souped-up.

OF THE WHEEL

Left Salvador Dali delivers a painting to an exhibition on a Graziella in 1967. Note the folding handlebar moustache.

One constant preoccupation has been to make the bike occupy less space than it normally does. There was, as we've seen, a flurry of nineteenth-century patents laying claim to inventing the first folder, but the first functional folding bikes were designed to be dropped by parachute in the Second World War. However, with the dominance of the car in the post-war period, and the emphasis on cycling for pleasure rather than transport, a desire for more easily portable bikes grew. The charming Italian Graziella of 1964, with its elegantly curving bottom tube/rear rack captures the sunlit optimism of the time. It is a bike for posing on the seafront in Cannes, or tying to the back of one's yacht. With its small wheels, and cheerful colours, it returns cycling to its initial childishness. Brigitte Bardot was hired to ride it in an advert. Salvador Dali had one.

Other manufacturers followed suit. Raleigh produced a folding version of the 20-inch wheel Raleigh Twenty Shopper, calling it the Stowaway, which sold from 1971 to 1984. For strength the main tube folded at an oblique angle, which made the bike not so much fold as twist in two. With its Sturmey Archer three-speed-hub and steel mudguards it was, however, very heavy. One carried it on a crowded tube train at one's peril.

The 1971 Bickerton addressed the weight problem by producing an aluminium folder which weighed less than 10 kg. It was advertised with the slogan 'Go bag a Bickerton' as it was small enough and light enough to be carried in a bag. In its unpainted aluminium it reflected the aesthetic of the Space Age. But folding it took a while, involving four knobs on the handlebars, one on the seat stem, and one on the main tube. People quipped that by the time you had folded it you had missed your bus. But it found its advocates. A 56-year-old English grandmother, Christian Miller, rode across America on a Bickerton publishing a book of her travels, and proving the usefulness of folders in long distance touring.

An alternative solution was provided with the Strida in 1987. Arising from Mark Sander's Masters project at the Royal College of Art, the Strida is effectively a triangular frame hinged at the top. The wheels sit at the bottom corners, the handlebar is at the apex, and the rider sits a little way down one side. A weight-saving and maintenance free belt drive provides power to the rear wheel. In addition the wheels are mounted on only one side, allowing punctures to be repaired without taking the wheels off. In some ways it has the appearance of a Penny Farthing, more so than a 'normal' compact, and some riders find the riding position difficult to get used to. Folded it looks more like a baby buggy than a bike.

Above An early Raleigh folder is squeezed into a boot in 1965. The wheels could be removed and used as earrings.

Right City workers doing a Le Mans start after finishing work in 2010.

Hence the eventual dominance of the Brompton folding bicycle among city commuters, designed by Andrew Ritchie, a Cambridge Engineering graduate. Its clever design has led to it becoming a worldwide success. In Japan it is seen as a fashion statement, with bikes being customised with titanium hinge clamps and leather mudflaps. One order came from an Antarctic scientist who wanted one to get around the South Pole.

Unlike other popular folders, the Brompton sticks resolutely to 16 inch wheels rather than 20 inch. And its frame folds twice: the rear wheel flipping underneath the chainwheel, the main tube then folding, bringing the front wheel back to the centre. Cleverly, the chainwheel now sits between the two folded wheels, so you don't get oil on your trousers. It's not quite the equal of the Featherstone Kite, but Caractacus Potts would be impressed.

GETTING FIXATED
RETROSPECTIVES ON SPOKES

One of the most fascinating things about cycling is that, despite over a hundred years of innovation – of pneumatic tyres, aerodynamics and carbon fibre – a bicycle still remains a very simple thing. And this is no more clearly evident than in the return to basics that has characterised bicycle fashion in the twenty-first century. Whereas the eighties and nineties saw the evolution of the mountain bike and a seemingly exponential explosion of gears (on some racers numbering up to 30), recent years have seen a return to the basic plan of the first Safety Bicycle, with a single-speed rear wheel, and minimum gadgetry, making cycling simpler, and more in touch with its roots.

Fixies, or single-speed bikes, are obviously not new, and for many years had a cult following among some cyclists. Track bikes often used a single fixed gear without a freewheel. The advantages were obviously to do with weight. Fixed-gear bikes did not require the gears, cable, levers, mounting lugs and so on that a geared bike needed. They were also used in Cyclo-ball (as you can imagine, football on bikes), bike polo or 'artistic cycling' where riders and bikes carry out athletic and gymnastic manoeuvres. The advantage of a fixed-wheel bike in this case was that a rider can shift their bike into reverse.

Some modern single-speed bikes do have a freewheel (allowing one to coast with the pedals not moving). But a 'pure' fixie allows no such thing, making strenuous demands of the rider. The obvious challenges they offer are in terms of safety and braking. One brakes by either slowing down pedalling, or in an emergency, shifting one's weight forward and stopping one's legs to make the rear wheel skid. (Best not to do this in front of a policeman though, as purists who completely forsake calipers are breaking the law, which requires a braking mechanism on both wheels.)

The advantages of single speed bicycles are both aesthetic and athletic. They are beautiful. Stripped of gears, mudguards and levers, they distil cycling to its essence, and the sublime geometry of the diamond frame. Early fixies thus recycled old racers - the Peugeots, Falcon Eddy Merckxs that had sat in a garage - or if you were lucky, a classic Italian like a Pinarello or an Olmo. Stripped of the encrustations of convenience, the sleek beauty of their designs shone through. Classic Italian road racing frames now sell online for thousands of pounds.

Athletically fixed gears also have a number of advantages. They force you to cycle at a certain intensity. When climbing a hill on a geared bike you have the option of shifting down the gears to maintain a decent pedalling cadence. But on a fixie you have to attack it with a certain velocity and momentum to maintain your pedalling speed. Otherwise you grind to a halt. Descending a hill on a fixed

The beauty of a fixie is its simplicity and for some reason this makes them more expensive!

hub also spins the legs – much as you would do on a spin bike in a gym – again increasing fitness and suppleness. And again on the flat: setting off requires a certain muscularity. If you want to be a picture of graceful cycling vigour, there is nothing better than standing poised at the traffic lights without putting your feet down – again easier on a fixed-wheel machine.

To this one can add a mechanical rationale for riding fixed. The chain is always in a straight line between front and rear cogs, so the transmission of power is always optimal. And without having to journey through a derailleur, friction is reduced to minimum. In terms of maintenance, a fixed wheel bike is the opposite of your 30-gear racer. A front caliper brake might need adjusting. One could put a little more pressure in the tyres. But apart from that there is nothing to do except polish it, and cycle.

It is also fair to say that cycling a fixie makes a statement. Many cyclists see themselves as part of a community, and loosely a movement, a reaction against firstly the car, but also the consumerism of modern life. Fixed wheel bikes are a

Below Having a trendy Hoxton beard to go with your fixie is not compulsory but it is desirable.

Right Fixie owners have a reputation, maybe undeserved, for wanting to let everyone know they have a fixie. Display stands are therefore optional.

way of saying 'less is more'. They insist that the value of cycling is not simply in terms of transport, but a rediscovery of the simple things: of fitness, efficiency and aesthetics in the simple lines of the design of the Safety Bicycle frame. They are their own time machines: denying the progress of the twentieth century, and returning to the halcyon days of the late 1800s. Gears in a sense represent a betrayal of the bicycle, a sense that somehow it isn't quite good enough, and pave the way to the car. Fixed gear bikes state that enough is good enough. As the French racer and writer, Henri Desgrange said in 1902 'I still feel that variable gears are only for people over forty-five. Isn't it better to triumph by the strength of your muscles than by the artifice of a derailer? We are getting soft... As for me, give me a fixed gear!'

ICONIC BIKES

The Chopper

When it burst onto playgrounds across the country in the early 1970s, the Chopper seemed like something from another planet. Its banana seat, ape hanger handlebars and Ford Capri-style central gear shift looked like a Curly Wurly-addicted adolescent's bicycling dream. Passing juveniles on space-hoppers would stop and stare.

But in fact the Chopper was a highly derivative, albeit highly successful bicycle. Its precursor was the American Schwinn Sting-ray, which came out in 1963, its design inspired by hot rod-style customized 'choppers' favoured by Hell's Angels.

Seeking to emulate Schwinn's success, Raleigh sent a designer, Alan Oakley, on a research trip to America. It is said he sketched the original design for the Chopper on the back of an envelope on the flight back. Whereas the Sting-ray echoed the curves of the original Schwinn cruisers, the Chopper offered a more angular, seventies design. Asymmetrically sized wheels were mounted on a triangular frame. A square-section rear tyre gave a dragster-style menace. A plushly upholstered banana seat echoed the outrageously curved handlebars. Big bold letters spelt out 'Chopper' on the main tube, as if there could be any question as to what kind of bike it was.

It was a hit with the kids. But not with the adults. Soon a spate of Chopper horror stories began to horrify middle England. The warning on the seat strap that 'THIS BICYCLE IS NOT CONSTRUCTED TO CONVEY PASSENGERS' was taken by some as inspiration, and playground pile-ups ensued. If seated too far back on the seat the front wheel could lift of the ground – fun for kids, but a major affront to bicycle safety campaigners. And downhill the small front wheel generated speed wobbles exacerbated by seventies flares. Gear knobs could be unscrewed, leaving a potentially painful protuberance in the event of a crash.

BRITISH
originality

Once there were ships. Then there were aircraft. Now there is Hovercraft, a whole new way of zipping across the sea – at high speed. It's this sort of original thinking that puts Raleigh out in front too, with innovations that really take off.

CHOPPER II

A fully-integrated design featuring hi-rise bars with height limiter; T-bar gear shift with visual indicator panel; 3-speed Sturmey Archer gear; and Raleigh cable brakes. Also foam-filled 'polo' saddle, prop stand and wide studded tread rear wheel tyre. Colours: Fizzy Lemon, Infra Red, Ultra Violet.

Some concessions to safety were made with the Chopper Mark II, introduced in 1972. The seat was moved forward to stop the front wheel lifting. And the handlebars were tilted forward and welded to the headpost, to stop kids angling them backwards, making the bike practically unsteerable. The result was a sort of forward-leaning Chopper, a push-me-pull-you of the bicycle world.

But the kid with the Chopper was still the coolest kid on the block. It rescued Raleigh, which had been struggling. By the end of the seventies, over 1.5 million had been sold. Apocryphal tales told of boys with hard-of-hearing parents who after being asked for a 'Chopper' for Christmas, bought him a shopper.

Other Iconic Bikes

'Omafiets' or Grandma bike
1892

Classy, stately, liberal and now newly revived by hipsters everywhere. Its sit-up-and-beg position is perfect for making sure you don't steer into a canal.

Specialized Stumpjumper
1981

Based on a design by Tom Ritchey, this was the first mass-produced mountain bike. It may have cost $750 dollars new, but it was available right off the shelf (if it hadn't sold out).

Avatar 2000
1980

One of the most famous and influential recumbents. Designed by David Gordon Wilson, an English-born MIT professor of engineering.

Lotus Type 108
1992

This all-conquering carbon-fibre time trial bicycle was manufactured by Lotus for Chris Boardman, who rode it to victory in the 1992 Olympic 4000m pursuit in Barcelona. It was designed by Mike Burrows and features an advanced aerofoil cross-section using a carbon composite monocoque frame.

Kuwahara E.T. BMX bike
1982

The director Steven Spielberg placed an order with this Japanese manufacturer for 40 BMX bikes to star in the film *E.T.* After the movie came out, Kuwahara started mass-producing replica *E.T.* bikes in their distinctive red and white livery.

TO INFINITY AND BEYOND
FLOATING, FLYING AND FUTURE BIKES

As an invention, the bicycle seems perfectly fitted to the human frame. Hands with opposable thumbs allow us to hold on and steer. Heads on top of our bodies provide a good view of the road. And bipedalism (walking upright) requires strong leg muscles as well as balance, again attributes ideally suited to the demands of cycling. As a result we can ride longer, faster and further than we could ever run.

But throughout the history of the bicycle, people have asked: do we need to stop there? Gears have multiplied our ability to travel at ever increasing distances and speeds (the speed record, with a car providing wind protection, stands at an incredible 167 mph/268 kph). But still, is travelling on land the sum of the bicycle's achievement?

Hence a number of thinkers have attempted to harness pedal power to more ambitious ends. For centuries, travelling by boat was faster than travelling by land, and inventors and thinkers have often tried to exploit pedal power on water. In 1895 the journal *Scientific American* asked optimistically whether there should not exist 'a machine of some kind that will be, in relation to water, what the bicycle is to land'.

The earliest attempts used inflated ribbed tyres both for flotation and propulsion, such as the Pinkert Navigating Tricycle, first piloted in 1894.

In 1883 an appropriately named Mr Ferry had crossed from Dover to Calais on another water tricycle, the weight of which caused it to be almost totally submerged. It required a tremendous effort to cover the twenty odd miles in the face of wind and tides. It was an amazing achievement, but more of a submarine than a water bike, and hence probably prone to rust.

Most modern versions of the floating bike effectively attach a bike to two kayaks to make a catamaran, the chain drive being re-routed to a propeller. The New Zealand made Akwakat allows you to bolt your own bicycle to its two inflated pontoons. A chain travels from the front chainwheel down to a coupling that drives a propeller at the back. The front forks bolt onto a rudder that steers from the front. One of the advantages of supplying your own bike is that you can keep your favourite saddle, handlebars and grips. You can even keep your front suspension for what it is worth.

Above Dunkirk Doughnuts – Georg Pinkert, of Hamburg, Germany with his 'nautical velocipede' or Navigating Tricycle which could travel on land and at sea.

Left April 1923: French inventor Alois Santa with his art nouveau bicycle aeroplane.

Covering greater distances using pedal power requires a more sophisticated approach, and a safer one: a vessel capable of dealing with high winds and rough seas. But pedal-powered boats – glorified pedalos – are capable of astonishing feats. The English explorer Jason Lewis was the first man to cross both the Atlantic and Pacific in a pedal-powered boat in 1995 and 2000. It was part of his human-powered (i.e. without motors or sails) circumnavigation of the globe, covering a total distance of 46,000 miles (74,030 km).

One of the greatest of human ambitions is to fly, and an even greater one being to cycle in the air – as happens in the most famous scene in the movie *E.T.*, when a boy on a BMX with an alien in the front basket takes off. Early HPAs (human powered aircraft) attempted to imitate birds with the arms being used to power the wings – what is referred to as an ornithopter, a flapping flying machine, such as that designed by Leonardo Da Vinci. They inevitably failed as the arms are not strong enough to create sufficient lift. But by using the larger muscles of the legs – the gluteus maximus and the quadriceps – a would-be cyclonaut stands a much better chance.

An early attempt was the Gerhardt Cycleplane of 1923, which had seven wings on top of each other attached to a balsa fuselage. The pilot's pedalling drove a two-bladed propeller. After being towed behind a car it achieved some short flights, but found it difficult to take off on its own. It is most famous for some newsreel footage showing it lifting momentarily off the ground before crashing, its stack of wings collapsing like a house of cards.

The first properly successful flying bike came in November 1961, when the Southampton University Man Powered Aircraft (SUMPAC) took to the air at Lasham airfield in Hampshire, flying 594 metres and achieving a height of 15

Left 'Phone home' – a still from *E.T.* (1982).

Right Gossamer Albatross over the English Channel, 12 June 1979.

feet. It was built of balsa and aluminium with a nylon skin, weighed 60 kg and had a 24-metre (80 ft) wingspan.

But the first winner of the Kramer Prize of £50,000 – for flying around a one mile figure-of-eight course – was won by perhaps the most famous HPA of modern times: Gossamer Condor. It was the brainchild of Paul MacCready and inspired by hang glider design. It had a wingspan of 30 metres (96 ft) and weighed just over 30 kg – only twice the weight of the average bike. Two years later a redesigned plane – the Gossamer Albatross – successfully flew across the English Channel in 2 hours and 49 minutes.

As lightweight materials like carbon fibre become more popular, and new discoveries such as graphene, which is 207 times stronger than steel, are more widely used, who knows what lies in store for the flying bike?

In 2013 the elegantly named AeroVelo Atlas won the $250,000 AHS Sikorsky Prize: for a human powered helicopter able to hover at an altitude of three metres for over a minute. It is every child's dream – a cross between a bicycle and a helicopter, the magical BMX of *E.T.* come true. But you will need a large garage to keep it in: it has four 33ft rotors, and an overall size of 47 metres (154 ft) – bigger than most commercial planes.

WHEN IS A BICYCLE NOT A BICYCLE?
STEAM, PETROL AND ELECTRIC POWER

When is a bicycle not a bicycle? When it is a motorbike. Or is it? For much of the century the line between bikes and motorbikes has been less distinct that it might at first seem. Motorbikes evolved from bicycles, and for many years they shared much with them – the frame design, the wheel size, the handlebars and saddle. Often engines were simply bolted on, leaving the pedals in exactly the same place. The earliest motorbikes, in this sense, were really motor-assisted bicycles.

In fact, the first motorised bicycle arrived soon after the invention of the bicycle itself. This was the French Michaux-Perreaux steam velocipede of 1868 – soon followed by an American version, the Roper Steam Velocipide of 1869 (although which came first is a matter of some contention). Instead of a bicycle computer, it sported a steam pressure gauge. Whether combining a highly pressurised steam engine with bicycling was a good idea or not is open to question. Certainly you might want to wear something a little more robust than a pair of cycle shorts.

A steam engine is an external combustion engine: heat is applied externally to a water-filled cylinder to create steam. They are bulky and dangerous because of the high pressures involved. An internal combustion engine, by contrast, provides combustion internally in the cylinder, through the explosion of an air–fuel mixture. They are lighter and more efficient, and better suited to smaller applications. So with the invention of the internal combustion engine in the 1880s the door opened to the first sensibly motorised bike, which can be seen in Daimler and Maybach's *Reitwagen* (riding car) of 1885. On its maiden outing it was ridden along the banks of the river Necker, reaching speeds of up to 7 mph.

Motorcycles went on to become more and more powerful. In 1901 Royal Enfield, previously a rifle and cycle manufacturer, introduced a motorcycle with a 150cc engine. Other manufacturers soon followed their lead – Triumph and BSA in the U.K., and Indian and Harley Davidson in the U.S. The First World War provided added impetus to production. The Triumph Model H became part of the war effort, featuring a 500cc single cylinder engine, belt drive and, significantly, no pedals.

It could be said that at this moment the motorcycle proper was born, and in a sense parted company with the humble bicycle. These were no longer assisted bicycles but *motorcycles*, a whole different proposition, capable of speeds beyond the reach of any frantic pedaller. A Brough Superior from the 1920s was capable of well over 100 mph. By the 1930s England boasted more than 80 motorcycle manufacturers.

Yet undeterred, a number of engineers and inventors remained faithful to cycling's original vision and continued to fit engines to bicycles. Partly cost was a consideration – an assisted bicycle required only a modest engine, sometimes as small as 25cc. Yet there was also a sense of attempting to preserve the economical and unobtrusive side of cycling, where an engine might be employed to ease one's progress up a hill, but downhill and on the flat, a pair of legs would do.

Perhaps the most famous of these curious hybrids is the French VeloSolex which was made between 1946 and 1988, and sold eight million bikes worldwide. Unlike a motorbike, the Solex had a 49cc engine over the front wheel. With a 1.25 litre petrol tank it could propel you 100 kilometres at speeds of up to 20 mph (35 kph). Rather than a clutch, you simply pulled a lever that lowered the engine

The VeloSolex smile: advertisement by René Ravo for VeloSolex c. 1950, with a one-year guarantee!

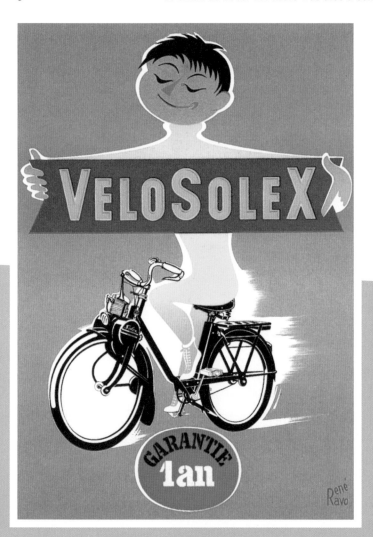

onto the front wheel, which it drove simply by friction. It became an iconic image on French roads. It had a starring role in Jaques Tati's 1958 film *Mon Oncle*. Advertisements showed fragrant young women on Solexes overtaking sweating racing cyclists on hills.

But probably the form of power most suited to the bicycle (other than legs) is electricity: like the bicycle itself, clean, silent and almost magical.

As early as 1885, Ogden Bolton patented an electrically assisted bicycle with a 10v hub motor – the standard form for most modern electric bikes. And soon other designs followed, such as the Humber Electric Tandem, which was exhibited at the Stanley Bicycle Show in November 1897.

One might ask why the electric bike didn't go on to prosper, given the availability of the technology. Here there are two answers: firstly, the popularity of the internal combustion engine – why bother with a new invention? The price of motorcycles and petrol was continually coming down. The other explanation is simpler. Although powering bikes by electricity was clearly viable, storing that power was a problem. A motorcycle could cheaply travel hundreds of miles – and then refuel. No battery-powered machine offered such range or flexibility.

But slowly electric bikes matured. The first viable models from the 1990s used heavy lead-acid car-type batteries – often the batteries weighing as much as the bike itself. Despite this the batteries were cheap to replace, being used in a variety of other vehicles, such as mobility scooters and golf-carts. Still the range was relatively limited, often little more than 10-15 miles.

However, in certain circumstances that could be enough. Early lead-acid electric bikes became tremendously popular in China. Bikes were already well established, following state subsidies in the 1950s. In the decade following 1998, sales of electric bikes and scooters grew from 56,000 annually to 21 million a year – more than twice the number of cars sold. It is estimated that there are 120 million electric bikes currently in use. Partly the reason for this growth was a deliberate attempt to ease congestion and pollution – banning cars and

Left A high-powered electric tandem of 1897.

Above right A crude but effective lead-acid electric bike in Shanghai, 2010.

motorbikes in city centres. It is no surprise that China is now the world's leading manufacturer of electric bikes, producing over 30 million a year.

But the truly liberating aspect of electric bike technology in the last ten years relates to batteries. Lead-acid batteries are cheap, but heavy, spending a lot of their energy in propelling themselves, let alone the bike or rider. With advances in battery technology in laptops and mobile phones a whole new range of batteries has become available. Lithium iron phosphate (LiFePO4) batteries are the latest offering, evolving from the hi-torque battery packs used to power cordless power tools. They are lightweight, have a longer life (up to 2,000 recharges) and because of their weight can be multiplied, giving bikes ranges of well over a hundred miles. But they are expensive: whereas Chinese lead-acid bikes are designed to be affordable to the masses, Lipo battery bikes are still a luxury product. A bike like the Haibike Xduro Hardnine electric mountain bike boasts a 36v crank drive motor and an 80 miles range. It may only cost 5 pence to recharge but it will set you back nearly three thousand pounds to buy it in the first place.

BITS THAT FELL OFF MY BIKE

When you're going on a long journey on your bike and you use your favourite panniers there's always some stuff that just won't fit in the right place. It's the same when you're writing a book, so here's some stuff that just wouldn't fit anywhere else but I still wanted to bring with me.

The Olympics

Currently cycling at the Olympics falls into four different areas: Track, Road, BMX and Mountain Bike. Only those first two appeared when cycling was one of the sports at the first modern games in Athens in 1896. It was here that Frenchman Paul Masson took three of the five golds on offer on the track by winning the Individual Sprint, the 1 km time trial and the 10 km. His compatriot Léon Flameng took the 100 km and the Austrian Adolf Schmal won the 12-hour race, covering a distance of 314.997 km. The only road race was over 87 km and was won by Greek rider Aristidis Konstantinidis.

The World Championships

The first world championships predate the Olympics and the UCI. They were organised by the International Cycling Association which had been the brainchild of Henry Sturmey, he of the three speed hub. Formed in 1892, the ICA held the World Championships the following year in Chicago. The competition had three events; One Mile Sprint, 10 km and 100 km. The American Arthur Zimmerman won the two shorter distances while Laurens Meintjes from South Africa took the stayers' race.

After the ICA fell apart following disputes between the member nations, the UCI was formed in 1900 and has held the World Championships ever since. There are events on the track and road as well as for BMX and Cross Country, as in the Olympics. In addition there are the lesser known *indoor* events of Artistic Cycling and Cycle-Ball. The former is the bicycling equivalent of gymnastics while the latter is, in effect, football on bikes but the ball is 'kicked' with one of the wheels or the rider's body.

Speed

As its name suggests, the International Human Powered Vehicle Association, IHPVA for short, is interested in human powered vehicles. Specifically, it encourages and sanctions attempts to push to the limits our ability to go faster under our own steam. Over the course of a week in September 2015, Dr Todd Reichert three times improved the record speed for a human powered bike over a flat 200 metre course. His quickest was 86.65 mph (139.45 kph) on 19 September.

With a little help, the quickest anyone has travelled on a bike is the 268.831 kph (167.044 mph) achieved by Dutchman Fred Rompelberg on 3 October 1995. Unlike Reichert, Rompelberg was paced, cycling just behind a motor dragster. This record stands as the Absolute World Speed Record for Cycling.

Fred Rompelberg getting up close and personal with a dragster while setting his cycling speed record.

With his total distance of 75,065 miles (120,805 km) Tommy Godwin could have made over twenty round trips between Paris and Moscow, or cycled to the moon in three years!

Distance

In 1939 a Brit named Tommy Godwin cycled 75,065 miles (120,805 km). This beat the previous record for distance covered in a single year by almost 10,000 miles! Cycling every day, which you would have to do in order to beat this record, you would need to cover over 205 miles (328 km) per day. Little did he know when he set off on his attempt on 1 January that nine months later Britain would declare war on Germany. By that time he'd almost completed 50,000 miles but was still about 15,000 miles short of the existing record. The Hun couldn't stop him and he carried on pedaling, beating Bernard Bennett's record on 26 October. War raged but the wheels kept turning, with his lights covered during blackouts. When the year ended and the record had been broken Tommy carried on pedalling because he had another record in his sights; the quickest cycle to 100,000 miles. He got there in May 1940!

Just last year the UltraMarathon Cycling Association announced that it would certify attempts at beating Godwin's record, and as this book goes to press two cyclists are in their saddles doing just that. In the UK Steven Abraham's 2015 effort is looking unlikely after he broke a leg in a collision with a car, but he is struggling on and began a concurrent attempt at the start of August. Over in the States Kurt Searvogel's attempt is still very much on target with an average of 208 miles (335 km) per day so far.

Cycling in Space

NASA's International Space Station orbits the earth at a height of around 256 miles (410 km) and travels round the earth in just over 90 minutes. With up to six astronauts on board it can be almost guaranteed that there is someone cycling at any given moment.

Astronauts need to exercise a lot more than we do on earth to maintain fitness. We get a lot of our fitness from everyday activities such as walking around, but this is not the case up there. Keeping fit in zero gravity is difficult because there is no force for the body to fight against. Muscle can deteriorate quickly and bones can weaken when they have nothing to do. One of the ways the astronauts counter this is on their stationary Station bike. It's not that dissimilar from one you'd find in a gym, although it is not solidly fixed to a surface so floats a little.

ACKNOWLEDGEMENTS

Like learning to ride a bike, putting a book together
involves a lot of falling off and getting back up again.
I fell off less because of the invaluable help of Katy
Denny, Jen Veall, Sally Bond and Michelle Mac.
Nicola Newman acted as a sturdy set of stabilisers
for us all. And my heartfelt thanks goes to you all.
I'd also like to thank Katie Cowan, the power behind
my saddle, who got me back on to an actual bike at
just the right time. Thanks too to Rooney the Border
Terrier for always thinking I'm ace. Keep pedalling!

PICTURE CREDITS

First published in the United Kingdom in 2016 by
Portico
1 Gower Street
London
WC1E 6HD

An imprint of Pavilion Books Company Ltd

ISBN 978-1-91023-256-9

A CIP catalogue record for this book is available from the British Library.

10 9 8 7 6 5 4 3 2

Reproduction by Mission Productions Ltd, Hong Kong
Printed and bound by Toppan Leefung, China

This book can be ordered direct from the publisher at www.pavilionbooks.com

Page 190 A little dog hitches a lift.

Below Prizewinners in the cycle parade at Devonport Dockyard Sports, Devon, 1923.